Option Valuation in the Presence of Market Imperfections

European University Studies
Europäische Hochschulschriften
Publications Universitaires Européennes

Series V

Economics and Management

Reihe V Série V
Volks- und Betriebswirtschaft
Sciences économiques, gestion d'entreprise

Vol./Bd. 1369

PETER LANG
Frankfurt am Main · Berlin · Bern · New York · Paris · Wien

Andreas Bell

Option Valuation in the Presence of Market Imperfections

PETER LANG
Frankfurt am Main · Berlin · Bern · New York · Paris · Wien

Die Deutsche Bibliothek - CIP-Einheitsaufnahme

Bell, Andreas:

Option valuation in the presence of market imperfections / Andreas Bell. - Frankfurt am Main ; Berlin ; Bern ; New York ; Paris ; Wien : Lang, 1993

(European university studies : Ser. 5, Volks- und Betriebswirtschaft ; Bd. 1369)

ISBN 3-631-45660-3

NE: Europäische Hochschulschriften / 05

ISSN 0531-7339

ISBN 3-631-45660-3

Printed in Germany 1 2 3 5 6 7

PREFACE

Option pricing theory is today becoming a part of every standard Finance course. Practitioners are routinely using the Black/Scholes valuation model as a benchmark. Yet, it is mostly being ignored that the so-called "Fair Value" of an option does not necessarily meet real market prices: The Black/Scholes pricing rationale is based on a perfect market environment that cannot be found anywhere in reality. Market participants who use theoretical pricing formulas or arbitrage relationships are often caught by market prices that significantly deviate from the output of the formula.

This thesis - written by Dipl.-Kaufm. Andreas Bell, MBA, in the course of a student exchange program between the Johann Wolfgang Goethe-Universität in Frankfurt and the University of Wisconsin in Madison - aims at bridging the gap between the ideal world of theory and market reality. The basis for the discussion is laid by a concise review of arbitrage bounds and the Black/Scholes pricing rationale. This is followed by a meticulous deliberation on various market imperfections that are encountered in reality and the impact they can have on option prices and their implied volatility. The reader will be surprised how many aspects, apart from the obvious fees and bid-ask spreads, may play a role. This is underscored by a comprehensive survey and discussion of numerous empirical tests academicians have carried out on the world's benchmark options exchange - the CBOE in Chicago. In connection with the significant and systematic deviations that are found, refinements of the Black/Scholes model (e.g. the Compound Option model, the Jump Diffusion model, and others) are discussed and tested. However, it is shown that they cannot consistently capture the pricing biases, either.

The work by Andreas Bell explains why option price deviations from model values that look like profitable arbitrage opportunities are mostly not exploitable when transaction costs and risks arising from market imperfections are taken into account. For the theoretician, the book offers a comprehensive discussion of the current academic work on the subject and stimulates the development of models that incorporate the real market environment. For the practitioner, the book provides indispensable insights that can prevent him from costly mistakes when evaluating strategies in the markets for derivative financial instruments.

Prof. Dr. Bernd Rudolph
Johann Wolfgang Goethe-Universität
Frankfurt, September 1992

ACKNOWLEDGEMENTS

I am grateful for the support of my thesis advisor, Prof. Alex Triantis of the University of Wisconsin, and for the fruitful and exciting discussions we had on the subject matter.

I wish to thank my parents and all other members of my family. Without their backing and encouragement, this work would not have been possible.

Similarly, I gratefully appreciate the advice and encouragement I received from the faculty of the Business School and from my fellow students.

Andreas Bell

Option Valuation in the Presence of Market Imperfections

TABLE OF CONTENTS

TABLE OF FIGURES

1. INTRODUCTION

The seminal work of Black and Scholes (1973) resulted in a major breakthrough for the solution of the option valuation problem. Merton (1973) complemented their work by formalizing a number of relationships between option values that arise from dominance arguments.

Triggered by the opening of the Chicago Board Options Exchange (CBOE) in 1973, options have become a widely used instrument among financial market participants. The growth of options markets and the proliferation of option related investment strategies has prompted extensive research in academia. Theoretical work has focused on the improvement and refinement of the Black-Scholes (BS) valuation concept. Empirical research has been conducted in order to assess the efficiency of options markets and the validity of valuation models.

The purpose of this thesis is to investigate the practical applicability of option valuation theory in light of the stringent assumptions it is based on. Trading in actual markets does not take place in the clean and frictionless environment that is a precondition for the bulk of option theory. A key concept in Finance that also forms the basis for most option valuation theory is the notion of <u>perfect markets</u>. In a perfect market, there are no fees or other transaction costs that might hinder investors from freely choosing and switching among securities. Securities with similar risk and return have the same price.[1] This price reflects the market's expectation of the security's future payouts and risk. Two subcomponents of perfect markets are market completeness and market efficiency. In a complete market, combinations of the existing securities allow the construction of any type of future payout across the future states of nature. In this respect, the introduction of new securities is therefore unnecessary.[2] Their payout and hence their value can be replicated by a combination of the already existing securities. Market efficiency requires that any information that could be used to predict the future price movement of a security is already reflected in its current price. This rules out risk-free profits from arbitrage opportunities. Security prices change in response to new information, which is random and unpredictable per definition, thus following a random walk.[3] (This will be readdressed in Chapter 4.1.)

This thesis presents and analyzes the various factors

---

[1] See Schmidt, Richard H.: Grundzüge der Investitions- und Finanzierungstheorie, Wiesbaden, FRG, 1983, pp. 45-46.

[2] See Ritchken, Peter H.: Options: Theory, Strategy and Applications, Glenview, Ill. 1987, p. 91.

[3] See Bodie, Zvi / Kane, Alex / Marcus, Alan J.: Investments, Boston 1989, p. 342.

that can influence option prices in actual markets. Their consequences for option market efficiency and their effect on the performance of alternative option valuation models will be discussed in depth.

The organization of the thesis is as follows: Chapter 2 presents the bounds and arbitrage relationships that have to hold for option prices in perfect markets in order to preclude riskless profits on zero investment. Chapter 3 presents option valuation concepts and examines the assumptions and intuition behind them. The arbitrage-based BS framework is shown to be the most appealing approach. Both Chapters 2 and 3 are not intended to extensively examine detailed aspects of the derivation of arbitrage relationships and valuation concepts. Rather, the material presented serves as a basis for the discussion in the subsequent chapters. Chapter 4 provides an extensive overview of features of actual markets that differ from theoretical assumptions, presenting an array of factors that can influence option prices by disturbing the prerequisites for arbitrage arguments. Chapter 5 addresses several important aspects that have to be considered in the context of empirical testing and market efficiency. Chapter 6 provides empirical evidence on how well the bounds and arbitrage relationships presented in

Chapter 2 actually hold. Chapter 7 discusses the real-market performance of the BS model, empirical findings about its systematic flaws, conceivable reasons for these defects, and approaches to mitigate them. In this context, the stock volatility implied in option prices plays a pivotal role. Chapter 8 presents several alternatives to the BS model that attempt to overcome its flaws by incorporating systematic changes in stock volatility. Whether these models actually perform better will also be discussed. In light of the findings and evidence presented, Chapter 9 assesses the limits to current option valuation theory when it comes to determining option prices in actual markets. Chapter 10 concludes the thesis.

A list of variables used in this work can be found in the Glossary. It also contains a list of abbreviations, especially those for academic journals.

2. ARBITRAGE BOUNDS AND RELATIONSHIPS IN PERFECT MARKETS

Option prices must comply with a number of dominance conditions. They have the form of bounds and relationships whose violation would make riskless arbitrage possible. In a frictionless environment, this would be a sign for serious inefficiencies in the markets.[4] Violations of these conditions are fairly easy to detect, and for any rational investor, regardless of risk preferences or wealth, it would be optimal to take an (even infinite) position in the offsetting portfolio to make a risk-free profit on zero net investment.[5] Such activities should drive option prices back within the bounds virtually at once.

In contrast to the arbitrage-based valuation models that will be introduced in the next chapter, the bounds and relationships do not require any knowledge of the underlying stock's volatility, and the arbitrage portfolio does not depend on continuous readjustment in order to maintain a riskless hedge. All that is required is that investors prefer more wealth to less. Hence, the conditions presented below depend on much weaker

[4] See Merton, Robert C.: Theory of rational option pricing, in: Bell Journal of Economics and Management Science 4 (1973), pp.141-183, here p. 143.

[5] See Bodie/Kane/Marcus: Investments, op. cit., p. 282.

assumptions than those required to determine exact option values by means of valuation models. Violations of the bounds and arbitrage relationships would therefore preclude any compliance of option prices with the much stronger assumptions that option valuation models are based on.[6]

In this chapter, the most important bounds and arbitrage relationships for options are presented. It should be pointed out that they do not take market imperfections such as fees, bid-ask spreads, nonsynchronous prices, etc. into account. These factors will be introduced in Chapter 4. Their effects on the strength of the bounds and arbitrage relationships have been examined in empirical tests and will be discussed in Chapter 6.

2.1. Lower Arbitrage Bounds

A thorough treatment of arbitrage bounds will be limited to those that have been subjected to rigorous empirical testing in the academic literature. For the sake of completeness, a supplement can be found in appendix 1.

---

[6] See Galai, Dan: A survey of empirical tests of option pricing models, in: Option Pricing: Theory and Applications, Heath 1983, edited by Menachem Brenner, pp. 45-80, here p. 50.

2.1.1. Minimum Value of a European Call

A lower bound inequality for a European call is

$$c \geq \max\ [0,\ S-Ke^{-rt}-PV(D)]$$

where c denotes the price of a European call, S is the current stock price, K is the striking price, r is the continuously compounded risk free rate of interest, and t is the time to maturity.[7] $PV(D) = \Sigma D_i e^{-rt_i}$, where i denotes the dividend payment dates until expiration, i.e. PV(D) is the present value of all the (assumed known) dividends to be paid before maturity. In words, the condition says that a European call must be worth at least the greater of zero or the stock price, minus the present value (PV) of the striking price, minus the PV of the dividends.

Proof:[8]

If $c<S-Ke^{-rt}-PV(D)$, buy the call, short the stock, and lend the PV of the striking price and the future dividends to realize arbitrage profits, as shown in the payoff table below.

[7] The actual expiration of an option is 10:59pm Central Time on the Saturday immediately following the third Friday of the maturity month. Trading ceases at 3pm Central Time on the last business day preceding the expiration date. To exercise the option, a customer must instruct his broker no later than 4:30pm on that day. Time to maturity is the calendar time until the Saturday of expiration.

[8] See Cox, John C. / Rubinstein, Mark: Options Markets, Englewood Cliffs 1985, p.130.

	payoff today	payoff at maturity $S^* \leq K$	$S^* > K$
buy call	$-c$	0	S^*-K
short stock	$+S$	$-S^*$	$-S^*$
lend Ke^{-rt}	$-Ke^{-rt}$	$+K$	$+K$
lend PV(D	$-PV(D)$	0^a	0^a
	>0	$K-S^*>0$	0

[a]PV(D) is liquidated as required to cover the cash dividends due from the short sale of the stock.
S^*denotes the stock price at option maturity.

2.1.2. American Calls and Early Exercise

Since American options can be exercised prior to the expiration date, they should never trade below intrinsic value (S-K), i.e. they must always be worth at least as much "alive" as "dead". If this relationship is ever violated, one can simply buy the call and make a profit by exercising it immediately, whereas this is impossible with European options. Hence, a lower bound inequality for an American call is

$$C \geq \max \{0, \max [\ S-K, S-Ke^{-rt}-PV(D)\ ]\}$$

where C denotes an American call. Since $S-K<S-Ke^{-rt}$, calls on nondividend paying stocks are always worth more alive than dead[9]. The only factor that can push the value alive below the value dead is dividends. Therefore, it can be

[9]Bodie/Kane/Marcus: Investments, op. cit., p. 596.

optimal to exercise an American call before expiration, which is called early exercise.

This feature gives rise to three important aspects that have to be recognized when working with American calls:

A) If <u>at all times</u> before maturity, PV(D) is less than the present value of the interest that can be earned on the striking price, the call should never be exercised early.

Proof:[10]

A loan of K today will be worth Ke^{rt} at expiration. Thus, the present value of the interest on the striking price is $e^{-rt}(Ke^{rt}-K)=K-Ke^{rt}$. Hence, if $PV(D)<K-Ke^{-rt}$ as required by the proposition above, then $S-Ke^{-rt}-PV(D)>S-K$. Since $C\geq S-Ke^{-rt}-PV(D)$, the value alive is greater than dead, i.e. $C\geq S-K$.[11]

However, it is not sufficient to check the early exercise possibility merely once. For example, if a major part of PV(D) pertains to a dividend that is paid long before expiration, PV(D) before its payment may be more than the present value of the interest on the striking price, but less at all times thereafter. This would

---

[10] See Cox/Rubinstein: Options Markets, op. cit., pp. 139-141.

[11] An information on ex-dividend dates is appropriate here. In reality, one has to exercise the option before the ex-dividend date in order to be included in the company's list of stockholders, thus being entitled to receive the dividend payment. The ex-dividend date is around two weeks before the payment date.

preclude optimal early exercise after that first dividend payment. Conversely, a single large dividend payment right before expiration will be worth more than $K-Ke^{-rt}$ at that date. But its present value may be less than $K-Ke^{-rt}$ if we compute these values 6 months before maturity (i.e. t=.5). It is therefore important to keep in mind that early exercise of an American call can only be precluded if $PV(D)<K-Ke^{-rt}$ <u>at all times</u>.

Whenever the PV(D) is more than the present value of the interest on K, early exercise <u>can</u> be optimal (but needn't always be), because the lower bound for the value alive lies below the exercise value S-K. On the ex-dividend date, S decreases by (approximately) D_i,[12] and consequently the intrinsic value S-K does the same.[13] The call value will abruptly go down at the ex dividend date if the only thing that had kept the market from pricing it at the lower "true" value had been the immediate exercise condition cum dividend, $C \geq S_{cum}-K$. In other words, the call value right after the dividend payment is the benchmark. If it is lower than the cum dividend stock price minus the

---

[12] The stock price can decrease by less than D_i due to tax influences. The dividend is taxed, but taxation of capital gains can be delayed indefinitely until the stock is sold. This disadvantage of dividend taxation will be reflected in a somewhat lower "dividend premium" that the market will assign to the cum dividend stock price. Hence, the stock price will go down by this lower amount when the stock goes ex dividend. Using the entire dividend when adjusting option bounds leaves something like a safety margin, should the market assign a "penalty" to the tax disadvantage that is close to zero.

[13] $S-K$ can now become $<S-Ke^{-rt}-PV(D)$, e.g. if $PV(D)=0$ because the dividend paid was the last one, but this is not the important point for this argument.

striking price, any investor is better off by exercising early.

In many cases, the ex-dividend call price will nevertheless be far higher, because the variability of the underlying stock may offer the prospect of ending up deep in the money. Valuation models and the variables that determine option prices will be discussed in Chapter 3.

B) The discussion above leads to another important proposition: A call should only be exercised right before an ex-dividend date or at expiration.[14] If early exercise is optimal, the call holder loses nothing by waiting until just before the dividend is paid, but gains the interest on the striking price that is earned in the meantime. Also, he can still change his decision about early exercise until then if the market should alter its evaluation of the call and push the price above S_{cum}-K. As discussed above, the "true" cum dividend call price right before the payment equals the benchmark ex-dividend call price. Hence, a call price above S_{cum}-K indicates that the call won't drop after the dividend payment.

This proposition can be employed in order to derive a tighter lower bound for n dividend payments, the so-called

[14] See Cox/Rubinstein: Options Markets, op. cit., p. 141.

pseudo-American lower bound:[15]

$$C \geq \max \{0, \max_{i} \{ [S-Ke^{-rt_i}-\sum_{j<i} D_{t_j} e^{-rt_j}], S-Ke^{-rt}-PV(D) \}\}$$

where t is the time to maturity, $t_1, t_2, \ldots\ldots, t_n$ is the vector of times to ex-dividend dates, and $D_{t_1}, D_{t_2}, \ldots\ldots, D_{t_n}$ are the respective cash dividend amounts (known in advance with certainty). In words, the bound shows that an American call cannot be worth less than the maximum of

i) the highest of the minimum values for otherwise identical European calls maturing right before each dividend payment, or

ii) the lower bound for an otherwise identical European call that is held until maturity.

Recalling the possibility of early exercise if $PV(D)>K-Ke^{-rt}$, it becomes obvious that early exercise is more likely the larger the dividend payment (=> PV(D) higher) and the closer to expiration a particular dividend payment is made (e.g. if one dividend D is paid a day before maturity, D will almost always be greater than the one-day interest on K, and hence $PV(D)>K-Ke^{-rt}$). Similarly, the exercise and hence also the early exercise of an option during its life is less likely the farther it is

[15] See Galai,Dan: Empirical tests of boundary conditions for CBOE options, in: JFEC 6 (1978), pp. 187-211, here pp. 191-192.

out-of-the money.[16]

By employing the insight that early exercise for calls will only occur right before the ex-dividend date, it is possible to confine the computation of $PV(D) \gtrless K-Ke^{-rt}$ to right before the ex-dividend dates instead of having to check for all times t. If we nonetheless want to check between the dates, the above stated allows the computation of a tighter condition for the preclusion of early exercise than stated in A). Let us assume that the nearest dividend payment will occur when T time to maturity is left. If for that date, $PV(D)_T < K-Ke^{-rT}$, the call won't be exercised before that dividend payment. Consequently, today with t>T, the values for the inequality above can be simply discounted back appropriately:

$$e^{-r(t-T)}PV(D)_T = PV(D)_t < e^{-r(t-T)}(K-Ke^{-rT}) = Ke^{-r(t-T)}-Ke^{-rt}$$

This procedure in effect eliminates the interest to be earned on the striking price until the nearest dividend is paid, because the call will rationally be exercised early only right before the payment: $(Ke^{-r(t-T)}-Ke^{-rt}) < (K-Ke^{-rt})$. This lower "present value of the interest on the striking price" is hence a more precise measure when contrasting it with PV(D) between dividend payments. However, as mentioned above, this check isn't even necessary for dates

[16] See Roll, Richard: An analytic valuation formula for unprotected American call options on stocks with known dividends, in: JFEC 5 (1977), pp. 251-258, here p. 252.

between dividend payments because early exercise can only be optimal right before a payment.

C) Finally, prospective dividend payments are the factor that determines the value of the early exercise possibility of American calls compared to their European counterparts. If it never pays to exercise early, this right must be worthless. Hence, the values of two otherwise identical American and European calls on a stock that with certainty won't pay any dividends must be equal.[17]

The rather elaborate discussion of the implications for call options that arise from dividends is necessary: as will repeatedly be seen in subsequent chapters, dividends and early exercise complicate the development of valuation models and cause problems in empirical testing.

2.1.3. Minimum Value of a European Put

A lower bound inequality for a European put is

$$p \geq \max\,[0,\ Ke^{-rt}-S+PV(D)]$$

where p denotes the price of a European put. This can be

---

[17] See Bodie/Kane/Marcus: Investments, op. cit., p. 596.

easily shown by means of a payoff table, along the same line of reasoning discussed for a European call. Therefore, this proof is omitted.

2.1.4. American Puts and Early Exercise

A lower bound inequality for an American put is[18]

$$P \geq \max\{0, \max[K-S, Ke^{-rt}-S+PV(D)]\}$$

The present value of dividends is added because their payment lowers the stock price appropriately, thus raising the value of the put. The reasoning behind this lower bound is similar to that employed for American calls. Again, the possibility to exercise before expiration will keep the market price at least at the put's intrinsic value K-S.

Three important features should be mentioned concerning American puts:

A) An American put should never be exercised early if PV(D) <u>is at all times</u> greater than the present value of the interest that can be earned on the striking price ($K-Ke^{-rt}$), because this results in K-S (value dead) being less than $Ke^{-rt}-S+PV(D)$ (minimum value alive).[19] Interestingly, this condition is exactly the opposite of the condition

---

[18] See Cox/Rubinstein: Options Markets, op. cit., p. 145.

[19] See ibid. p. 147.

that precludes early exercise of an American call.

B) If $PV(D)<K-Ke^{-rt}$ at a particular time, early exercise when the put is in-the-money may be optimal (if its "true" value is less than the intrinsic value). When exercising a put early, one gets the interest on the striking price right away, i.e. there is no specific event to await at which the benefit from early exercise can be optimally captured (in contrast to calls, where early exercise is carried out to get a dividend payment, and was shown to be optimal only right before it). Hence, within the time periods where $PV(D)<K-Ke^{-rt}$, rational early exercise of American puts cannot be pinned down to specific dates.

C) Unless it is sure that $PV(D)>K-Ke^{-rt}$ at all times before maturity, the right to exercise an American put early must clearly have value, thus raising its price above that of its European version.

Since rational early exercise can't be confined to specific dates and can never be ruled out for non-dividend paying stocks or after the last dividend has been paid, the academic literature displays a widespread avoidance of puts as far as the testing of valuation models, market efficiency and arbitrage bounds is concerned.

2.2. European and American Put-Call Parity

One of the most prominent arbitrage relationships is the so-called put-call parity. It arises from the fact that a call can be replicated by taking an appropriate position in the corresponding put (with the same striking price and time to maturity) as well as the stock and riskless T-bills. (They should mature at the same time as the option, as will be elaborated in Chapter 5). Of course, the parity allows not only the replication of the call, but of any one of the four securities employed by taking the appropriate position in the other three. For European options, the put-call parity condition is[20]

$$c=S+p-Ke^{-rt}-PV(D), \text{ or equivalently } p=c-S+Ke^{-rt}+PV(D).$$

This again can be proved using a payoff table:

	payoff today	payoffs at maturity $S^*\leq K$	payoffs at maturity $S^*>K$
portfolio A:			
buy call	$-c$	0	S^*-K
portfolio B:			
buy stock	$-S$	$+S^*$	$+S^*$
buy put	$-p$	$K-S^*$	0
borrow Ke^{-rt}	$+Ke^{-rt}$	$-K$	$-K$
borrow PV(D)	$+PV(D)$	0^a	0^a
		0	S^*-K

[a]The loan of PV(D) is paid back until maturity by using the dividends paid out by the stock.

[20]See Ross, Stephen A. / Westerfield, Randolph W.: Corporate Finance, St. Louis 1988, pp. 511-513.

Since the payoffs of both portfolios are the same at maturity, their prices at the outset must also be equal. If this relationship is ever violated, arbitrage should drive the prices back into line.

The put-call parity has resulted in some well-known option jargon. Writing a call and hedging with the replicating position by buying the put, buying the stock, and borrowing $Ke^{-rt}+PV(D)$ is called a "conversion" of a put into a call. Conversely, writing a put against the replicating position of long the call, short the stock, and lending $Ke^{-rt}+PV(D)$ is called a "reversal".[21]

The above considerations must be amended for American options. If for all times before maturity, early exercise of both the call and the put could be ruled out, the European put-call parity would still be valid for them. However, this is not possible. If early exercise of the call can be ruled out because at all times, $PV(D)<K-Ke^{-rt}$, this condition at the same time makes optimal early exercise of the put possible. Therefore, while the early exercise feature of the call is worthless, the American put price will be higher than that of its European

[21] See Gladstein, Mathew L. / Merton, Robert C. / Scholes, Myron S.: The returns and risks of alternative put option portfolio investment strategies, in: JOB 55 (1982), pp. 1-55, here p. 16.

counterpart.[22] Hence, the European version of the parity turns into an inequality: $P \geq C - S + Ke^{-rt} + PV(D)$.
Conversely, if $PV(D) > K - Ke^{-rt}$ at all times, the above line of reasoning is reversed, resulting in a higher American call price and yielding: $P \leq C - S + Ke^{-rt} + PV(D)$. However, this is not very realistic because the preclusion of early put exercise would require a dividend payment coinciding right with the expiration date. If for some time until maturity, $PV(D)$ is greater than $K - Ke^{-rt}$, but for some time smaller (e.g. after the last dividend payment), both the call and the put might be exercised early. Hence, both American options will be worth more than their European version. However, this does not in any way imply that equality in the put-call parity will be restored.

The magnitude of P being greater or smaller than the portfolio on the right hand side is bounded by arbitrage arguments. Eventually, the possibility of early exercise results in a band. The general relationship is given below without proof:[23]

$$C + K + PV(D) - S \geq P \geq C + Ke^{-rt} - S \; .$$

This band does not take into account that perhaps only one of the two options (put or call) might be exercised early

---

[22] See ibid. p. 5.

[23] See Cox/Rubinstein: Options Markets, op. cit., p. 152.

(as discussed above). In that case, one side of the band is less tight than actually determinable.

2.3. The Box Spread Arbitrage Relationship

A spread is a combination of two or more calls (or two or more puts) on the same stock with different exercise prices or times to maturity. A vertical spread is a long position in one option combined with a short position in another option on the same stock, but with a different exercise price.[24] A horizontal or time spread involves options with different expiration dates.

The box spread is a position formed by simultaneously purchasing a bullish vertical call spread (long the call with the lower striking price, short the call with the higher striking price) and a bearish vertical put spread (long the put with the higher striking price, short the put with the lower striking price).[25] All four options of course have the same time to expiration, and the two different striking prices are the same for the calls as for the puts.

As is proved by the payoff table below, the box spread

---

[24] See Bodie/Kane/Marcus.: Investments, op. cit., pp. 574-575.

[25] See Ronn, Aimee G. / Ronn, Ehud I.: The box spread arbitrage conditions: theory, tests and investment strategies, in: The Review of Financial Studies 2 (1989), pp. 91-108, here p. 92.

position (for European options, or alternatively when early exercise can be ruled out) is equivalent to riskless lending:[26]

	payoff today	payoffs at maturity $S^*<K_1$	$K_1 \le S^* \le K_2$	$S^*>K_2$
buy $c(K_1)$	$-c(K_1)$	0	S^*-K_1	S^*-K_1
short $c(K_2)$	$+c(K_2)$	0	0	K_2-S^*
short $p(K_1)$	$+p(K_1)$	S^*-K_1	0	0
buy $p(K_2)$	$-p(K_2)$	K_2-S^*	K_2-S^*	0
		K_2-K_1	K_2-K_1	K_2-K_1

Regardless of the terminal stock price, the payoff from the box spread is K_2-K_1 at expiration. Therefore, the position should be worth exactly the present value of K_2-K_1 at the outset when European options are used:

$$c(K_1)-c(K_2)-p(K_1)+p(K_2) = (K_2-K_1)e^{-rt}$$

With American options, the possibility of early exercise implies the prospect of premature repayment of the synthetic loan at par. Hence, the box spread must cost <u>at least</u> as much as the present value of K_2-K_1, thus changing the equality to a greater than or equal to inequality:[27]

$$C(K_1)-C(K_2)-P(K_1)+P(K_2) \ge (K_2-K_1)e^{-rt}$$

Whenever the box spread costs less than the riskless lending position, arbitrage profits can be made in perfect markets by simply buying the box spread and borrowing

---

[26] ibid. p. 93.

[27] See ibid. p. 93.

$(K_2-K_1)e^{-rt}$ at the riskless rate.

Empirical testing of the box spread arbitrage condition will be addressed in Chapter 6.

2.4. The Call Convexity Condition

Call prices are a convex function of the striking price for options with identical maturity that are written on the same underlying stock.[28]

If $K_2 = \lambda K_1+(1-\lambda)K_3$, with $K_1<K_2<K_3$,

where $\lambda=\frac{K_3-K_2}{K_3-K_1}$ and $(1-\lambda)=\frac{K_2-K_1}{K_3-K_1}$ and $0\leq\lambda\leq1$, then the following condition for the respective calls must hold:[29]

$$C(K_2) \leq \lambda C(K_1)+(1-\lambda)C(K_3)$$

The following proof is for European calls and for American calls if the stock pays no dividends before maturity, thus precluding rational early exercise. If in violation of the condition, $C(K_2)$ sells for more than the convex combination of the other two calls on the right hand side of the inequality, a butterfly spread (long $\lambda C(K_1)$ and $(1-\lambda)C(K_3)$, short the intermediate call) offers riskless arbitrage profits, as shown in the payoff table below:[30]

---

[28] See Bhattacharya, Mihir: Transactions data tests of efficiency of the Chicago Board Options Exchange, in: JFEC 12 (1983), pp. 161-185, here p. 165.

[29] See Cox/Rubinstein: Options Markets, op.cit., p. 133.

[30] See ibid. p. 135.

	payoff today	payoffs at maturity: $S^* \leq K_1$	$K_1 < S^* \leq K_2$	$K_2 < S^* < K_3$	$K_3 \leq S^*$
short $C(K_2)$	$+C(K_2)$	0	0	K_2-S^*	K_2-S^*
long $\lambda C(K_1)$	$-\lambda C(K_1)$	0	$\lambda(S^*-K_1)$	$\lambda(S^*-K_1)$	$\lambda(S^*-K_1)$
long $(1-\lambda)*$ $C(K_3)$	$-(1-\lambda)*$ $C(K_3)$	0	0	0	$(1-\lambda)*$ (S^*-K_3)
	>0	0	$\lambda(S^*-K_1)$	$\lambda(S^*-K_1)$ $+(K_2-S^*)$ >0 [31]	0

Along similar lines, the convexity condition can be proven for puts.[32] Also, it can be shown that the call convexity condition still holds for American calls if the stock pays dividends before maturity, thus possibly prompting early exercise.[33] However, the proof of this fact is omitted because it would not enhance our understanding of the basic concept.

The call convexity condition results in a relationship between call prices that causes them to appear as a convex curve across striking prices, as shown in Figure 2.a. below:

[31] This must be greater than zero and is proved in Cox/Rubinstein p. 134.

[32] See Cox/Rubinstein: Options Markets, op. cit., p. 145.

[33] See Galai, Dan: A convexity test for traded options, in: Quarterly Review of Economics and Business 19 (1979), pp. 83-90, here p. 89.

Figure 2.a.: The call convexity condition

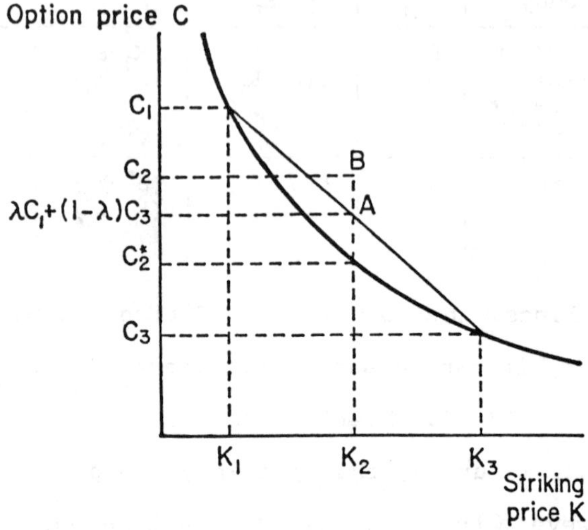

(from: Galai, Dan: A convexity test for traded options, in: Quarterly Review of Economics and Business 19 (1979), pp. 83-90, here p.85.)

If $C(K_2)$=A on the line $\lambda C(K_1)+(1-\lambda)C(K_3)$ in the figure above, the call prices still conform to the convexity condition. If $C(K_2)$ is above that line, say at B, then a sure, immediate profit of at least B-A can be made.

It should be noted that apart from convexity, the exact shape and position of the curve is not implied by the convexity condition. For this, a valuation model is necessary. Valuation models are presented in the following chapter, while empirical tests of the call convexity condition will be addressed in Chapter 6.

3. OPTION VALUATION FRAMEWORKS

Option valuation models are theories that determine an appropriate theoretical value of an option so that it is consistent with the price of the underlying stock.[34] However, it is important to point out that model values are not necessarily equal to market prices. None of the models can be established without making numerous assumptions about several of the following: the perfection of the market, the behavior of interest rates and the stock's volatility, or the risk preferences and utility functions of the investor. When trying to apply a theoretical model to the real world, it becomes immediately clear that virtually none of these assumptions can actually hold.

Thus, in actual markets, option prices are first and foremost determined by supply and demand, just like prices for everything else. This supply and demand is influenced by the imperfections of the market environment, such as taxes, fees, bid-ask spreads and so on (Chapter 4 will take a close look at these factors). Anything that affects investors' trading decisions but is not in the model tends

---

[34] See Figlewski, Stephen: What does an option pricing model tell us about option prices?, in: FAJ (September/October 1989), pp. 12-15, here p. 12.

to push the market price away from the model value.[35] But this does not necessarily reject the validity of the model under the assumptions that are required for it to hold. Despite these problems, traders actually use valuation models as a pricing equation, but more like a rule of thumb rather than an exact formula that produces the appropriate price in a given market situation.[36]

In this chapter, the most important approaches to option valuation are presented. In depth aspects of their mathematical derivation are usually omitted because that is not the focus of this thesis. All of the models assume perfect markets. The material presented below in this chapter serves as a basis for the subsequent discussions in the context of the imperfect trading environment that is found in reality. Chapter 4 contrasts model assumptions with the market environment and discusses transaction costs and other market imperfections that are encountered in actual trading. Chapters 8 and 9 present empirical evidence on the performance of valuation models. Also, they will introduce a number of alternative models with relaxed or altered assumptions compared to the basic cases that are discussed below.

---

[35] See ibid. p. 12.

[36] See ibid. p. 14.

3.1. Binomial Option Valuation

Only a brief overview of the derivation of the binomial model is given. The purpose of its introduction is to concentrate on the important aspects of its methodology, assumptions and variables in order to point out the relationships to the Black-Scholes formula that will be discussed thereafter.

3.1.1. Derivation of the Formula

Let's assume we know that the stock price will either go up or down in the next period, realizing a return of u or d, respectively. We can then replicate the payoff from a call option by forming a portfolio containing Δ shares of stock and the amount of B in riskless bonds, where R is one plus the riskless rate for one period.[37]

The stock path is:

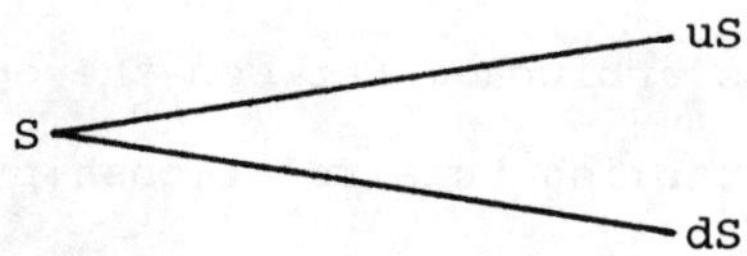

[37] See Cox, John C. / Ross, Stephen A. / Rubinstein, Mark: Option pricing: a simplified approach, in: JFEC 7 (1979), pp. 229-263, here p. 232.

The corresponding option path is:

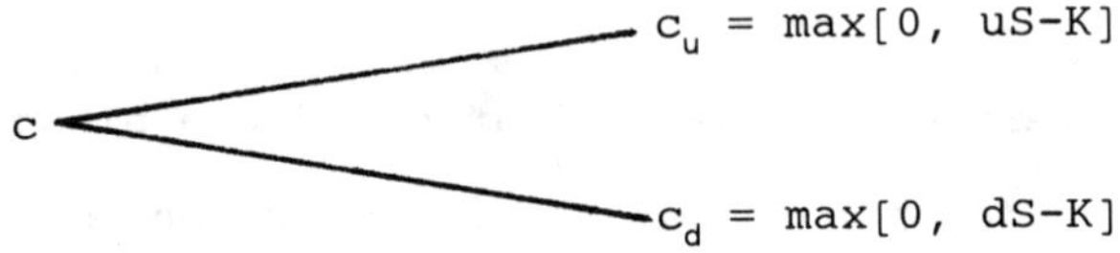

The path of the replicating portfolio is:

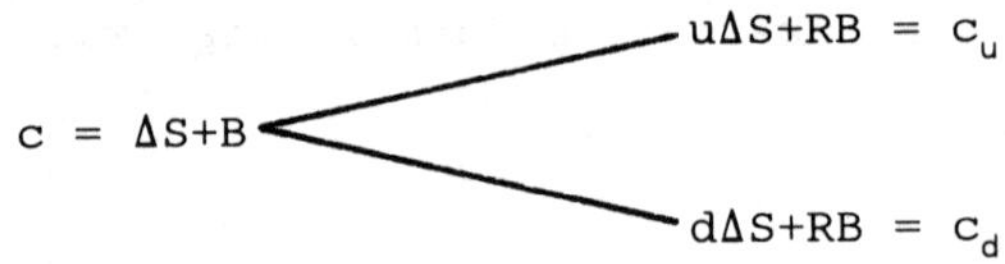

Solving the two linear equations on the right hand side of the figure above for Δ and B yields:

$$\Delta = \frac{(c_u - c_d)}{(u-d)S}$$

$$B = \frac{(uc_d - dc_u)}{(u-d)R}$$

In order to preclude riskless arbitrage, it must be true that the replicating portfolio costs just as much as the call:[38]

$$c = \Delta S + B$$

In perfect markets, riskless arbitrage between the option and the portfolio will reestablish this relationship if a violation should occur. For calls, B is always negative, which means that the call can be replicated by holding Δ shares of stock and borrowing B at the riskless rate.

---

[38] See ibid. p. 234.

By introducing $p=\frac{(R-d)}{(u-d)}$ and $1-p=\frac{(u-R)}{(u-d)}$ as the so-called "pseudo-probability" of going up or down (which is merely a mathematical construct, and not a true probability to compute an expected value), the relationship can be rewritten as:

$$c = \frac{[pc_u+(1-p)c_d]}{R}$$

This valuation formula always has to hold for European calls in perfect markets. For American calls, however, it is only valid if C>S-K because of their early exercise feature (if the value for C should turn out to be less than this intrinsic value, arbitrage will prevent the American call from dropping below S-K). As was pointed out in Chapter 2, C is always greater than S-K in the absence of dividends. Binomial valuation with dividends will be addressed later. The same method can be used to value (European) puts, which will be replicated by shorting stock and lending.[39]

The binomial approach can be easily extended to more than one period. The result is a binomial "tree" for the stock and hence for the respective option path.

---

[39] See ibid. p. 258.

Figure 3.a. below depicts a three-period binomial tree for the option price:[40]

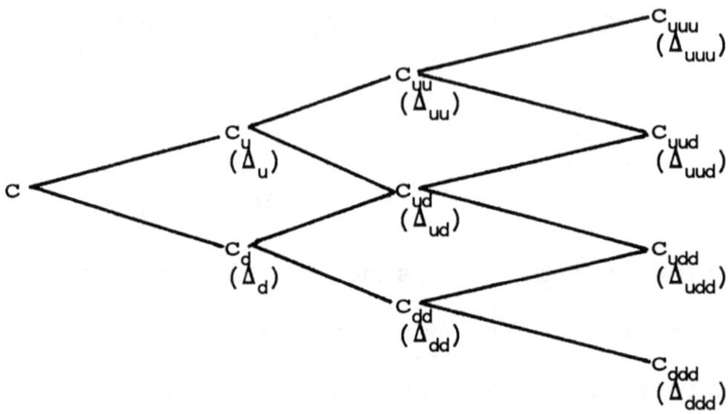

The Δs in parentheses show the respective fraction of shares held at any particular point in the replicating portfolio. The possible stock values in the third period that are produced by the corresponding stock tree determine the possible values for the option at expiration in the third period. These expiration values are then used to find the initial option value c by solving the tree backwards with the formula given above.

A general, n-period formula can be derived to value the option (but this is not the subject of this discussion). It uses the initial stock price and the striking price as direct input variables and captures the recursive

[40] See Bodie/Kane/Marcus: Investments, op. cit., p. 618.

computation of the tree in a closed-form solution.[41]

3.1.2 Assumptions and Information Requirements

In order to determine the option value with the binomial model, the initial stock price S, the striking price K the riskless return R per period and the magnitude of the stock's up or down return (u,d) have to be known, as does the number of periods.[42] It is important to point out three important implicit assumptions connected with this approach:

1. The use of the riskless return per period (R) implies that the risk-free interest rate that will prevail over the life of the option is known and <u>constant</u>.[43] Also, borrowing and lending rates are equal.
2. The magnitude of the up or down return (u,d) of the stock until the option's expiration is also assumed to be known and constant. This is equivalent to assuming a constant stock volatility.[44]
3. The fraction of the stock to be held in the replicating

---

[41] See Cox/Rubinstein: Options Markets, op. cit., p. 178.

[42] See ibid. p. 173

[43] In more sophisticated binomial models, the interest rate can also be a deterministic function of time.

[44] Again, more sophisticated binomial models do allow the return u and d to be a deterministic function of time.

portfolio (Δ) assumes that shares are divisible.

3.1.3. Risk-Neutral Valuation

The binomial model displays all of the intriguing features of arbitrage-based option valuation models. First of all, it is not necessary to know the probability of the stock's up or down movement, and hence its expected rate of return. Therefore, any subjective notions different investors might have about the underlying stock's future return are not necessary to value the option.[45] Regardless of investors' differing expectations, they will all arrive at the same option value.

Second, the only assumption necessary about an investor's behavior is that he prefers more wealth to less wealth and thus has an incentive to pursue arbitrage profits.[46] The same formula is obtained regardless of risk preferences because investors' attitudes towards risk are not a required variable for valuation by means of replication. The value of the call must be the same for any set of preferences, including risk neutrality, because the arbitrage argument with the replicating portfolio

[45] See Bodie/Kane/Marcus: Investments, op. cit., p. 615.

[46] See Cox/Rubinstein: Options markets, op. cit., p. 173.

always holds.[47] In fact, the pseudo-probability p is the true probability that the stock will go up if investors were risk neutral (i.e. indifferent between a certain return and an uncertain return with the same expected value). Using this risk-neutral stock movement probability p, the call's expected future value can be determined. Its value today is equivalent to this expected future value, discounted at the riskless rate in a risk-neutral world.[48]

Third, the stock price itself is the only random variable on which an option depends.[49] This is a good explanation for the fact that the stock's expected return doesn't influence the option value, as mentioned above. In effect, the current stock price already incorporates investors' views about its future return, as well as other variables such as the covariance with the market, expected cash flows or the market price of risk.[50] By the same token, the call value is not directly dependent upon the random prices of other securities or portfolios such as the market portfolio, which is the cornerstone of the

---

[47]See Cox, John C. / Ross, Stephen A.: The valuation of options for alternative stochastic processes, in: JFEC 3 (1976), pp. 145-166, here p. 153.

[48]See Ritchken, Peter H.: Options, op. cit., pp. 104-105.

[49]See Cox/Rubinstein: Options Markets, op. cit., p. 174.

[50]See Merton, Robert C.: On the pricing of contingent claims and the Modigliani-Miller theorem, in: JFEC (5) 1977 pp. 241-249, here p. 242.

capital asset pricing model.

The bottom line is that risk attitudes and characteristics of assets other than the underlying stock can influence option values only indirectly, through effects on the variables used in the model. But they are not separate determinants of the option value.[51]

3.1.4. Adjustment of the Replicating Portfolio

As already indicated by the changing Δs, the composition of the replicating portfolio requires readjustment after each period according to the realized position in the binomial tree. This readjustment is vital in order to maintain a riskless hedge if one wants to realize riskless arbitrage profits from a mispriced option by taking an offsetting position in the replicating portfolio.

The fraction of stock to be held, Δ, is called the hedge ratio of the option, indicating the change in the option's price for a $1 increase in the stock price.[52] For calls as well as puts, Δ rises when the stock price rises, and falls when the stock declines.[53]

---

[51] See Cox/Rubinstein: Options markets, op. cit., p. 174.

[52] See Bodie/Kane/Marcus: Investments, op. cit., p. 599.

[53] Although this might not be obvious for puts, it is nonetheless true because the put's Δ is negative (stocks are shorted). The higher the stock price, the less stocks are shorted, thus implying a higher Δ because of the negative sign.

When replicating a call for arbitrage purposes, the readjustment makes it necessary to buy additional stock and finance it by additional borrowing if the stock price has gone up in the previous period. Conversely, stock is sold and the money is employed to partly repay the loan if the stock price has gone down.[54] The value of the portfolio at the end of a period is always exactly sufficient to pay for the adjustments that are necessary for the following period, i.e. the adjustment does not require the investor to put up any additional money.[55]

The viability of such a dynamic replication strategy will be the subject of further discussion in subsequent Chapters. It should be emphasized at this point that transaction costs will have a significant impact because they are incurred repeatedly due to the necessary portfolio adjustments.

---

[54] If the arbitrage is conducted to take advantage of an underpriced call by buying it and shorting the corresponding replicating portfolio, the positions in stocks and bonds are of course exactly reversed, i.e. stocks are shorted according to Δ and the money is partly invested in bonds according to B.

[55] See Cox/Rubinstein: Options markets, op. cit., p. 176.

3.1.5. Dividends and Early Exercise

The binomial model can cope with dividends and the early exercise feature of American options. As was pointed out in Chapter 2.1.2., early exercise of calls is only optimal right before an ex-dividend date. Assuming that the period of an expected dividend payment as well as its amount is known, the stock price is adjusted accordingly at that point in the stock path.[56] When solving the corresponding option tree backwards, the value dead before the stock goes ex dividend is used as the value of the option for any point in the tree at the dividend payment date if the value alive would be less. This implies early exercise at that point, right before the dividend is paid. Obviously, this method requires one to actually go through the whole tree. A simple adjustment in the general binomial formula that would allow a closed-form solution is not possible.[57]

---

[56] See ibid. p. 242.

[57] See ibid. p. 240.

Figure 3.b. below is an example for a stock path with a fixed dividend payout of D at the end of the second period:

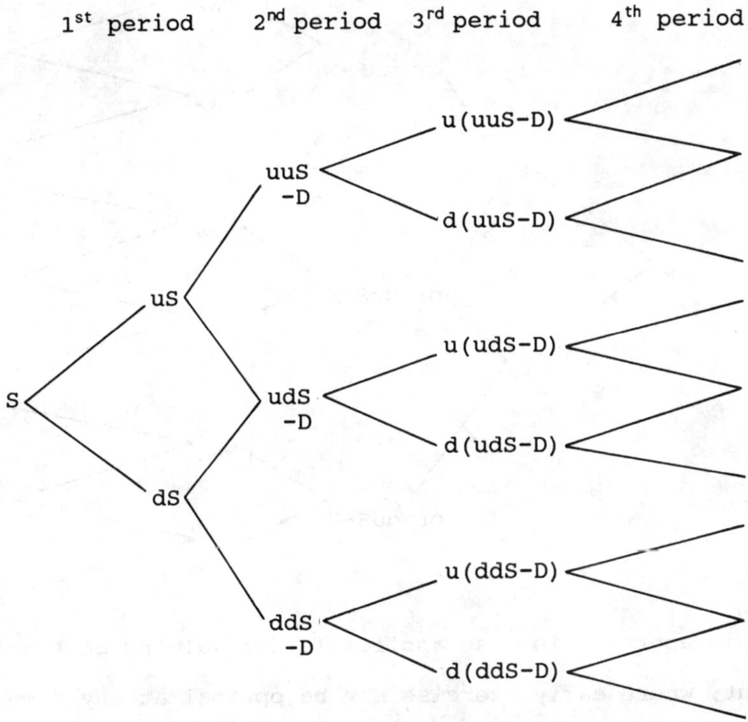

Figure 3.c. shows the corresponding option:

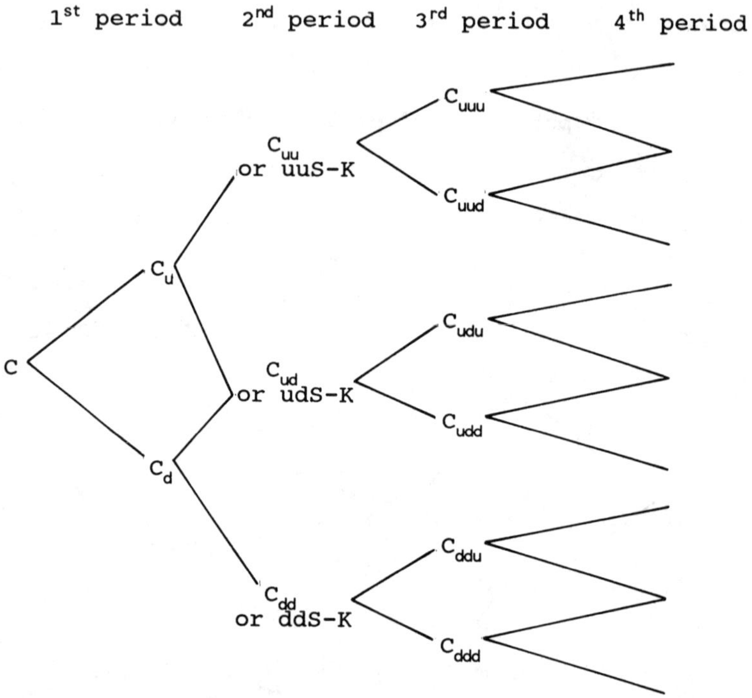

This approach is also applicable for valuing an American put, where early exercise may be optimal at any time, especially in the absence of dividends.[58]

Notice that the branches of the trees do not meet after the ex-dividend date. They do meet as usual if the stock pays a fixed dividend <u>yield</u> δ instead of a cash

---

[58]See Cox/Ross/Rubinstein (1979): op. cit., p. 258.

dividend.[59] For European options, the absence of early exercise makes it therefore possible to simply adjust the binomial formula if a constant dividend yield is paid out. In this case, the initial stock price is replaced with $s(1-\delta)^n$, where n is the number of ex-dividend dates until maturity.[60] However, fixed dividend yields do not rule out early exercise of American options, thus making it still necessary to actually go through the whole tree to value them.

3.2. The Black-Scholes Model

Although the Black-Scholes (BS) is a much more prominent valuation formula than the binomial approach, the assumptions and features connected with binomial option valuation have been presented rather extensively. The reason for this is that the BS model can be viewed as a logical extension of the binomial case, as will be discussed. It therefore displays basically the same features, relies on comparable assumptions, and is based on the same line of reasoning: arbitrage-based valuation by means of replication.

---

[59] See Cox/Rubinstein: Options markets, p. 242.

[60] See Cox/Ross/Rubinstein (1979): op. cit., p. 256.

3.2.1. Functional Form

The Black-Scholes option valuation formula is:[61]

$$c = SN(d_1) - Ke^{-rt}N(d_2)$$

with

$$d_1 = \frac{\ln(\frac{S}{K}) + (r + \frac{1}{2}\sigma^2)t}{\sigma\sqrt{t}}$$

$$d_2 = d_1 - \sigma\sqrt{t}$$

where

- r = the annualized continuously compounded risk free interest rate that prevails during the life of the option.
- σ = standard deviation of the expected annualized continuously compounded rate of return (CCRR) of the stock. Throughout this thesis, σ is meant when "stock volatility", "stock price volatility" or simply "volatility" is mentioned without further elaboration.
- $N(d)$ = probability that a standardized normally distributed random variable will be less than or equal to d (cumulative normal density function).

Just like the binomial model, the Black-Scholes formula determines the value of a call by valuing the corresponding replicating portfolio, where

$$N(d_1) = \frac{\partial c}{\partial S} = \Delta_c$$

---

[61] See Black, Fischer / Scholes, Myron: The pricing of options and corporate liabilities, in: Journal of Political Economy 81 (1973), pp. 637-659, here p. 644.

is the call's hedge ratio. It is always positive between $0 \leq \Delta_c \leq 1$ and denotes the fraction of shares to be held. $Ke^{-rt}N(d_2)$ is the amount to be borrowed at the riskless rate.[62]

By solving the European put-call parity for the put price, the value of European puts can also be determined. Substituting the BS call formula for the call price in the parity results in a direct BS put formula:[63]

$$p = Ke^{-rt}N(-d_2) - SN(-d_1)$$

Here, $-N(-d_1) = \frac{\partial p}{\partial S} = \Delta_p$ is the put's hedge ratio. Being always negative between $-1 \leq \Delta_p \leq 0$, it denotes the fraction of shares shorted per put.[64] $Ke^{-rt}N(-d_2)$ is the amount to be invested in bonds at the riskless rate.

Besides indicating the stock fraction in a replicating portfolio, the hedge ratio for puts and calls is also the partial derivative of the option price with respect to the stock price. When the stock moves $1, the option moves $Δ. Of course this is only exact for infinitely small changes, because the hedge ratio also changes when the stock moves, thus triggering the portfolio readjustment.

An offsetting position of 1 call short and Δ shares

---

[62] See Cox/Rubinstein: Options markets, op. cit., p. 205.

[63] See ibid. p. 211.

[64] See ibid. p. 212.

long is an example of a neutral hedge.[65] By continuously adjusting the position according to changes in Δ, any movements in the stock price are neutralized by exactly the opposite movement in the option. Hence, the hedged position is riskless and should consequently earn the riskless rate.[66]

3.2.2. Assumptions and Information Requirements

The Black-Scholes model relies on several restrictive assumptions:[67]

1) Markets are perfect, there are no margin requirements, taxes or transaction costs.

2) The stock pays no dividends (the basic formula does not take dividend payments into account, nor does it capture the early exercise problem).

3) If the option is a put, it must be European to rule out early exercise (American calls will not be exercised early in the absence of dividends).

4) The stock price is lognormally distributed with known and constant volatility.

5) The market operates continuously, and hence the stock

---

[65] See Black, Fischer: Fact and fantasy in the use of options, in: FAJ (July/August 1975), pp. 36-72, here p. 39.

[66] See Black/Scholes (1973): op. cit., p. 641.

[67] See Ross/Westerfield: Corporate Finance, op. cit., p. 519.

price moves continuously, i.e. there are no jumps.

6) The risk free interest rate is known and constant.

Black and Scholes assume that a particular process governs the movement of the stock price. It is a so-called Wiener process with certain drift component, also known as geometric Brownian motion. Formally, a stock's return that accords to geometric Brownian motion is given as

$$\frac{dS}{S} = \mu dt + \sigma dz$$

where μ is the instantaneous mean, σ is the instantaneous volatility, and dz is the Wiener process. The stochastic term, σdz, is independent of its value in other periods and has a mean of 0 and variance of $\sigma^2 dt$. Consequently, if the stock moves in continuous time (infinitesimally small time increments), the percentage change in the stock value is <u>normally</u> distributed with mean μdt and variance $\sigma^2 dt$, i.e. the mean and variance are proportional to the time increment.[68] Thus, as the time increment gets ever smaller, the possible stock price movement within this increment is also very small. Hence, jumps in the stock price are ruled out. After discrete (finite) time intervals, Geometric Brownian motion results in a

[68] See Cox/Ross (1976): op. cit., p. 146.

lognormal distribution for the stock price.[69]

When analyzing the BS formula, a comparison with the binomial approach is useful. In the BS model, σ replaces the magnitude of the stock's up or down return as a measure of stock volatility. The continuously compounded riskless rate r replaces the per period interest rate R, and the time to maturity t replaces the number of periods n. However, these replacements do not alter the basic implications that arise from the character of the input variables when compared to the binomial approach. The 5 input variables in the BS model rely on the same assumptions that were pointed out after the introduction of the binomial model in Subsection 3.1.2.: known and constant interest rate, known and constant volatility,[70] and divisibility of shares. Like the binomial model, the BS model employs the concept of risk-neutral valuation and requires the adjustment of the replicating portfolio.

The main difference is that the derivation of the BS model depends upon the assumption of continuous trading and a lognormal stock price distribution. It can be shown that these two assumptions are also a limiting case of the binomial approach. When the number of periods n within a

---

[69] See Black/Scholes (1973): op. cit., p. 640.

[70] As in the binomial case, more sophisticated versions of the BS model allow a slight departure from these assumptions by letting interest rates and volatility be a deterministic function of time.

given time to expiration t approaches infinity in the binomial tree, the range of possible stock prices at option maturity expands and ultimately takes on a lognormal distribution.[71] Obviously, this requires that stocks are traded continuously, with a new price being generated in every infinitessimally small time increment.

Clearly, a lognormal stock price distribution is a more appealing assumption than the limitation to two possible outcomes in every period of the binomial model. But whether lognormality really holds in reality is not clear at all. Also, it is doubtful whether actual markets offer the opportunity to trade continuously. A related point is that continuous trading also requires that the replicating portfolio be continuously adjusted. The assumption of constant stock volatility is also stringent. In addition, there is the question of where and how to get the best estimate for this variable. While S, K and t are known and the short term interest rate r over the life of the option can be observed (although its stationarity is also questionable), the future stock volatility σ is <u>not</u> observable. Chapter 4 will contrast the BS assumptions with market reality. Obviously, the volatility is the big unknown that causes many of the problems when valuing

---

[71] See Cox/Ross/Rubinstein (1979): op. cit., p. 250.

options with the BS model.[72] It will hence repeatedly be the focal point of the discussion in subsequent chapters.

3.2.3. Dividends and Early Exercise

The original BS formula only holds when the underlying stock does not pay any dividends, and for puts only when the option is European (to preclude early exercise). In the case of continuously paid proportional dividends (fixed dividend yield), an adjustment to the formula is possible for European options by discounting the initial stock price with the expected dividend yield, here shown for calls:[73]

$$c = Se^{-\delta t}N(d_1) - Ke^{-rt}N(d_2)$$

$$d_1 = \frac{\ln\left(\frac{Se^{-\delta t}}{K}\right) + \left(r + \frac{1}{2}\sigma^2\right)t}{\sigma\sqrt{t}}$$

$$d_2 = d_1 - \sigma\sqrt{t}$$

where δ is the annualized continuously compounded dividend yield. If fixed cash dividends are expected, one can reduce the stock price by their present value, but this approach already produces merely a close, but inexact

[72] See Black (1975): op. cit., p. 36.

[73] See Merton (1973): op. cit., p. 171.

approximation.[74]

The complications that arise from early exercise when valuing American calls in the BS framework cannot be captured by simply adjusting the stock price. For American calls, a widely used approximation is the pseudo-American call value. It is a straightforward application of the pseudo-American lower bound that was introduced in Chapter 2. As mentioned there, early exercise of American calls is only optimal right before the dividend is paid. We can thus approximate the value of an American call on dividend paying stocks with the following method:[75]
We compute the BS values of European options that expire right before each one of the ex-dividend dates that occur during the life of our American call. For each of these European calls, we adjust the stock price by subtracting the present value of those dividends that are paid before the respective maturity date. We also compute the value of a European call that expires at the same time as our American call if held to maturity, again subtracting the present value of the dividends from the current stock price. The highest of the computed European option values

---

[74] See Cox/Rubinstein: Options Markets, op. cit. p. 269.
Comment: This inaccuracy can be shown by employing a binomial tree. The correct tree with cash dividend payments at the true dates has branches that don't meet thereafter. It yields a slightly different European option value than the approximation tree where the starting stock price is reduced by PV(D), leaving the branches connected.

[75] See Black (1975): op. cit., p. 41.

is our approximation for the value of the American call.

The pseudo-American method assumes certain early exercise before one of the dividend payments, or no early exercise. This ignores the opportunity of the true American call holder to decide at each ex-dividend date whether to exercise or not, depending upon the then-prevailing stock and option price. Reflecting this opportunity, the actual American call value will be higher than the pseudo-American approximation.[76] Thus, dividends cause the following relationship between option values:

adjusted European ≤ pseudo-American < American

More sophisticated models for valuing American calls with known dividends will be addressed in Chapter 7. To date, no closed form solution for dividend-unprotected American puts has been found.[77] Geske (1978) has found a way to incorporate stochastic dividend yields in the valuation of European options.[78] However, to date no option valuation model can handle uncertain future cash dividends.[79]

---

[76] See Geske, Robert / Roll, Richard: On valuing American call options with the Black-Scholes European formula, in: JOF 39 (1984), pp. 443-455, here p. 444.

[77] See Galai (1983): Survey, op. cit. p. 70.

[78] See Geske, Robert: The pricing of options with stochastic dividend yield, in: JOF 33 (1978), pp. 617-625.

[79] See Galai (1983): Survey, op. cit., p. 49.

3.3. Option Sensitivities

For a better understanding of option price behavior and the replicating strategy, it is useful to examine the sensitivity of option values to changes in one of the five BS variables. Below, three important sensitivity relationships that are repeatedly readdressed in this thesis are presented.

a) The hedge ratio as a function of the stock price:
As defined earlier, the option's hedge ratio Δ is the fraction of shares to be held or shorted in the replicating portfolio. It is also the partial derivative of the option price with respect to the stock price. Graphs for the hedge ratios of calls (Δ_C) and puts (Δ_P) are given below. As mentioned before, $0 \leq \Delta_C \leq 1$ and $-1 \leq \Delta_P \leq 0$. The graphs point out that the hedge ratio changes the most when the stock moves if the option is at-the-money. Hence, portfolio rebalancing for at-the-money options is especially crucial.

Figure 3.d.: Δ_c and Δ_p as a function of the stock price

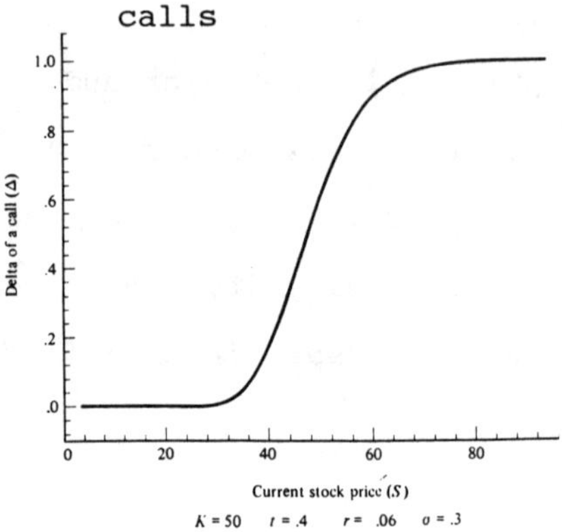

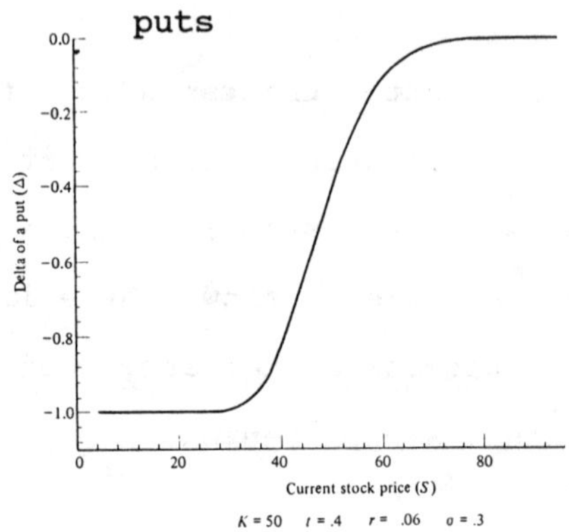

(from: Cox, John C./Rubinstein, Mark: Options markets, Englewood Cliffs 1985, p. 222+226.)

The behavior of the hedge ratio has an important implication: Someone who replicates a call will buy more shares as the stock rises. Someone who replicates a put will short more shares when the stock falls. In short, if markets are inefficient enough to let investors have an impact on prices, those investors who construct synthetic options through replication might exacerbate the stock price movement that prompted their action, possibly even triggering a vicious circle. As will be shown in Chapter 4.9., the existence of traded options can alleviate this market impact.

b) The sensitivity of an option to changes in the stock volatility, examined as a function of the current stock price:

Let us define the sensitivity of an option to volatility changes as the option's Λ (Lambda). For calls, $\Lambda_c = \frac{\partial C}{\partial \sigma} > 0$ and for puts, $\Lambda_p = \frac{\partial P}{\partial \sigma} > 0$. The Lambda of both calls and puts is always positive.[80] This is straightforward because the higher the volatility, the higher the probability to end up deep in the money. This prospect is especially important when the option is at-the-money, i.e. when the stock price is close to the striking price. Hence, Lambda is greatest for at-the-money options. The resulting graph for Λ as a function of the stock price is similar for both calls and puts.

Figure 3.e.: Λ as a function of the stock price

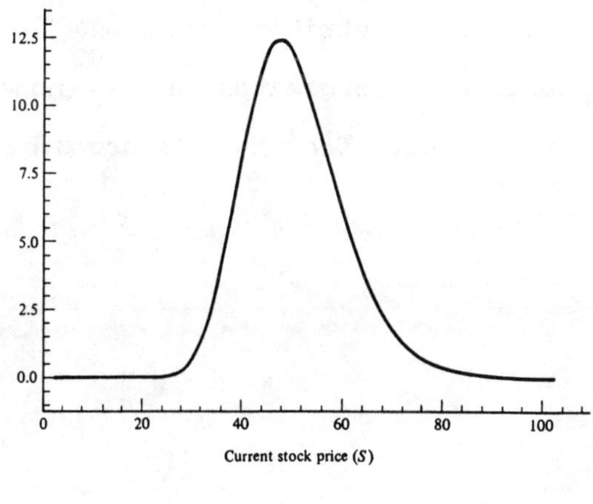

(from: Cox, John C./Rubinstein, Mark: Options markets, Englewood Cliffs 1985, p. 225.)

---

[80] See Cox/Rubinstein: Options Markets, op. cit. p. 229.

c) The reaction of the option price to changes in the interest rate:

$\frac{\partial C}{\partial r} > 0$, that is the call price rises if the interest rate rises, assuming the stock price remains unchanged. This is straightforward, because the present value of the striking price (Ke^{-rt}) falls when the interest rate rises, thus moving the call closer to or further into the money. The sensitivity as a function of the stock price is greatest for at-the-money calls, and the resulting graph is similar to that of Δ_c (therefore, it is not repeated; see Figure 3.d.).[81]

$\frac{\partial P}{\partial r} < 0$, that is the put price falls if the interest rate rises. Again, this can be explained by the effect of the falling present value of the striking price (Ke^{-rt}). As with calls, the sensitivity is greatest at the money, and the graph is similar to that of Δ_p (see Figure 3.d.).[82]

---

[81] See ibid. p. 226.

[82] See ibid. p. 233.

3.4. Preference Based Valuation

3.4.1. The Black-Scholes Framework with Constant Proportional Risk Aversion and Discrete Trading

Although the problems associated with the stringent assumptions in the BS model will be examined in greater depth in the next chapter, it is convenient to allude to the discussion of continuous trading at this point. In practice, it is clearly not possible to continuously rebalance the replicating portfolio. One obvious reason for this is that markets are closed at night and over the weekend. Hence, the accumulation of information can cause jumps in the stock price. An adjustment at discrete intervals makes any arbitrage between the portfolio and the option risky because of the resulting hedging errors. This destroys the basis for the arbitrage based approach to option valuation (except if the hedging errors are uncorrelated with the market and hence diversifiable; this point will be elaborated in Chapter 4.2.).

However, it is possible to "save" the Black-Scholes formula in a discrete trading framework under otherwise unaltered assumptions if investors are assumed to display a particular form of risk aversion. If the utility of investors is constant proportional risk averse (CPRA),

Rubinstein (1976) shows that the BS formula still holds even if only discrete-time trading is possible.[83] A constant proportional risk averse investor is equally averse towards losing a particular fraction of his wealth (proportional risk) regardless of his absolute amount of wealth. For example, he will assess the risk to lose $1 of his $10 total wealth equal to losing $100,000 if he was a millionaire. One of the utility functions that displays CPRA is logarithmic utility of wealth.[84]

3.4.2. Valuation in Incomplete Markets

3.4.2.1. Market Completeness and the Economic Role of Options

One of the primary prerequisites for the approaches to option valuation discussed so far is market completeness. As pointed out before, any type of payout across the possible future states of nature can be constructed if the market is complete, thus providing the basis for valuing new securities (e.g. options) by means of replication. A precondition for market completeness is that there exist as many "different" securities as future states of the

[83] See Rubinstein, Mark: The valuation of uncertain income streams and the pricing of options, in: The Bell Journal of Economics 7 (1976), pp. 407-425, here p. 408.

[84] See Pratt, John W.: Risk aversion in the small and in the large, in: Econometrica 32 (1964) pp. 122-136, here p. 134.

world.[85] Different means that the security's payoff pattern across states cannot be replicated by a portfolio formed from the other securities. This prerequisite is plausible because linear algebra shows that one always needs as many variables (securities) as equations (states) to come to a single solution.

If the market is complete, any payout pattern that is not provided by one of the existing securities can be achieved by a combination of them. In particular, it is possible to create the payoff of any state-contingent claim, which is a security that pays $1 in one distinct future state but $0 in all others.[86] Consequently, it is also possible to infer the current price of these claims or any other additional security, e.g. an option. If we only assume that investors prefer more wealth to less wealth and hence have an incentive to pursue arbitrage profits, the price of the additional security must be equal to that of the portfolio. This is the principle of risk neutral valuation that has been discussed earlier. Obviously, risk neutral valuation depends on market completeness.[87]

---

[85]See Cox/Rubinstein: Options Markets, op. cit., p. 432.
Comment: The only possibility to get around this requirement is completion by dynamic portfolio adjustment, as shown later.

[86]See Ritchken: Options, op. cit., p. 95.

[87]See ibid. p. 106.

Market completeness is not only a convenient environment for the valuation of options. It also has an economic implication that makes it desirable to pursue it. For one, a complete market offers any conceivable payout pattern an investor might desire, thus providing optimal conditions for an individual's wealth allocation decisions. More importantly, an economic theorem states that complete markets are always Pareto-efficient (not to be confused with the informational efficiency defined in the introduction). Pareto-efficient financial markets are desirable because they imply that no other set of securities can make investors better off without making at least one investor worse off.[88] The problem with options that arises when markets are assumed to be complete is a lack of economic rationale for their existence. They would merely duplicate payout patterns that could already be produced without them.[89] It should not be forgotten, however, that even in complete markets options can still be useful if they provide these patterns at lower (transaction) costs, lead to a faster and wider dissemination of information, or serve as an implicit predictor of future events (e.g. their price could imply anticipations of stock volatility, dividends and interest

---

[88] See Cox/Rubinstein: Options Markets, op. cit., p. 435.

[89] See Ritchken: Options, op. cit., p. 91.

rates).[90] If markets are incomplete, options could also serve as a provider of new payout patterns.

It can be shown that puts and calls written on the individual existing securities can complete the market.[91] However, their introduction is not always sufficient to guarantee market completeness. Ross (1976) proves that puts and calls traded on a single portfolio can complete the market, even in cases where options on the individual securities can't.[92] The precondition is that the securities forming the portfolio can be combined in such a way that the portfolio's payoff is different in every state. This result provides an important economic rationale for options: market completion. In particular, it suggests that this task may be accomplished better by using index options (assuming the index can differentiate among all states) than by introducing a long list of puts and calls on individual securities.[93]

The major problem with this environment, of course, is that risk neutral valuation of those options seems impossible. However, the possibility of replication adjustment can alleviate the problem to some extent. The

---

[90] See Cox/Rubinstein: Options Markets, op. cit., p. 444.

[91] See Ritchken: Options, op. cit., p. 99.

[92] See Ross, Stephen A.: Options and efficiency, in: Quarterly Journal of Economics 90 (1976), pp. 75-89, here p. 84.

[93] See Cox/Rubinstein: Options Markets, op. cit., p. 441.

discussion of the binomial model at the beginning of this Chapter showed that a portfolio formed by combining two different securities in fixed proportions (stocks and riskless bonds) can replicate the payoff from an option after one period if there are only two possible states (uS and dS). This is logical because the market is complete, with as many securities as future states of the world, but the confinement to two states of the world is highly unrealistic. However, even with multiple states, it is still possible to preserve market completeness and hence the principle of valuation through replication if there are possibilities to readjust the portfolio before the respective future states occur. The binomial trees show that with one adjustment, the option payoff in three different states can be reproduced. With two adjustments, five different states can be spanned, and so on.[94]

Consequently, frequent trading can be a surrogate for additional securities in order to complete the market, thus preserving option valuation through replication. But despite its theoretical appeal, this solution has some flaws that should be pointed out. Obviously, the market completing function of options would be lost again. Also, the time horizon for the future states has to be long enough to accommodate some readjustment periods in

---

[94]See ibid. p. 443.

between, although this is theoretically no problem in the world of continuous trading and instantaneous time intervals. But as will be discussed in greater detail in the next chapter, continuous trading is not feasible in the real world and causes considerable transaction costs.

Therefore, an option valuation approach that does not try to circumvent incomplete markets, but deals with them directly, is presented below.

3.4.2.2. A Valuation Approach in Incomplete Markets

If the market is incomplete and can't be completed by means of portfolio adjustment, the option valuation framework based on replication does not hold. However, Ritchken (1985) has derived bounds on the option price in such an environment by means of linear programming. The presentation at this point is not meant to be a detailed description of his derivation. Rather, the bounds are introduced in order to illustrate the effects that the omission of a single BS assumption can have.

The stock price S and the price of a risk free pure discount bond that pays \$1 at maturity, $B=e^{-rt}$, is assumed to be observable. B is also the sum of the current prices e_j of all state-contingent claims, i.e. $B=\sum_{j-1}^{n} e_j$, because it will be worth \$1 in all future states at time t with certainty. This relationship relies on the simple assumption that investors prefer more wealth to less, thus implying they will pay the same price for the same payout pattern if arbitrage profits are to be precluded.[95] The prices e_j cannot all be inferred from existing security prices because the market is incomplete, and hence they become the decision variables in the following linear programming problem:[96]

$$\max \text{ (or min) } C = \sum_{j-1}^{n} C_j e_j$$

$$\text{subject to} \quad S = \sum_{j-1}^{n} V_j e_j$$

$$B = \sum_{j-1}^{n} e_j = e^{-rt}$$

$$e_j \geq 0$$

where V_j is the future stock price in state j and $V_1 \leq V_2 \leq \ldots\ldots \leq V_n$. The maximization problem computes an upper bound and the minimization problem a lower bound on the call price under these constraints. The resulting lower bound is

$$C_{min} = \max\ [0,\ S-Ke^{-rt}]$$

which is identical to the lower arbitrage bound without

---

[95] See Ritchken, Peter H.: On option pricing bounds, in: JOF 40 (1985), pp. 1219-1233, here p. 1226.

[96] See ibid. p. 1222.

dividends for European calls that was introduced in Chapter 2.[97] This result could be expected because of the no arbitrage assumption made about the investors' risk preferences. Obviously, this lower bound is not very tight.

The upper bound is:[98]

$$C_{max} = S - \frac{KS}{V_n}$$

where V_n is the largest possible future stock price. Its tightness depends heavily on the size of V_n.

Tighter bounds can be derived in the same fashion when further restrictions are imposed. It is possible, for example, to impose the restriction of risk aversion, with investors valuing payouts in lower states of aggregate wealth higher than the same payout occurring in a high wealth state. This implies that a low wealth state-contingent claim will cost more than a high wealth state claim, even if the ex ante probability of their respective future state to occur is equal.[99] If each ex ante probability is provided, the price of each state-contingent claim must be equal to that probability, divided by a discount factor that reflects the time value

---

[97] See ibid. p. 1225.

[98] See ibid. p. 1224.

[99] See Ritchken: Options, op. cit., p. 96.

of money as well as the risk preferences of the investors. With risk aversion, those discount factors increase with increasing aggregate wealth. With the discount factors as decision variables, this relationship between them can be used as a restriction in a linear programming problem to obtain tighter bounds.

Their derivation is not the purpose of this section. The point is that the bounds can be influenced depending on the assumed risk preferences of investors and the probability distribution of the underlying securities.[100]

The discussion of linear programming bounds indicates the problems for option valuation that arise when the replication argument is given up. Apart from the observed stock and bond price, the linear programming approach requires the following information:

1. The number of mutually exclusive and exhaustive future states (n) is known.
2. The future value V_j of the stock in every one of these states is known.
3. The ex ante probability of the states' occurrence is given (if risk preferences are considered).
4. The risk preferences of the investors can be quantified in terms of the price they would assign to a state-contingent claim according to the aggregate wealth of the

---

[100] See ibid. p. 107.

future state in which its payout of $1 occurs.

Clearly, these information requirements are overwhelming. In addition, only bounds are obtainable, i.e. it is not possible to derive an exact option price.

3.4.3. The Black-Scholes Framework versus Preference-Based Valuation

Non-replication based valuation models can work within less stringent assumptions than the BS framework requires. However, the two approaches discussed above have been presented in order to point out that this comes only at an expense. In one case, an assumption is merely replaced by another, i.e. CPRA replaces continuous trading. In the case of preference-based bounds, the complete omission of one assumption (no market completeness, not even with dynamic readjustment) can only be dealt with by requiring an array of additional information.

In the face of these results, the question remains whether preference-based valuation can ever be a useful and practical alternative to the BS model. The remaining chapters of this thesis will, therefore, address the market environment found in reality and discuss the approaches that have been proposed to adjust the BS framework to it.

4. THE MARKET ENVIRONMENT IN REALITY

Real markets have little resemblance to the ideal conditions assumed for the arbitrage relations in Chapter 2 or the Black-Scholes valuation framework in Chapter 3. An abundance of transaction costs and trading limitations can be found, coupled with fluctuations in interest rates and the question of how stock prices are really distributed.

This chapter gives an overview of the factors that might cause observed option prices to deviate from their theoretical values. The subsequent chapters will address pricing biases and empirical tests. They will draw heavily on the information presented here in order to justify observations, concepts and results.

4.1. The Distribution of Stock Prices

In an efficient market, security prices fully reflect all available information. If markets are efficient, the prices are believed to follow a random walk, or more precisely, they are outcomes of Martingale processes. Martingale processes allow for positive expected price changes as a compensation for the time value of money and systematic risk.[101] Nonetheless, the expected future price is independent of past prices of the security.[102] When security prices are outcomes of Martingale processes, this is commonly referred to as the random walk hypothesis. (Strictly speaking, true random walks would be more restrictive because in contrast to general Martingales, they require successive stock returns to be not only independently, but also identically distributed.[103] This would imply that the distribution parameters can never change.) One point must be mentioned here that will be readdressed in greater detail in Chapter 6: it is consistent with market efficiency and the random walk hypothesis to observe slight violations of the random walk, i.e. there can be some incidences where not all information is already reflected in the prices. The reason is that speculators must be rewarded with sufficient returns for the costs incurred and work required to trade those deviations away.[104]

There are many different probability distributions that would be consistent with the random walk hypothesis.[105]

---

101 See Bodie/Kane/Marcus: Investments, op. cit., p. 342.

102 See Smidt, Seymour: A new look at the random walk hypothesis, in: JFQA (1968), pp. 235-261, here p. 235.

103 See Bodie/Kane/Marcus: Investments, op. cit., p. 342.

104 See Smidt (1968): op. cit., pp. 236-237.

105 See Smidt (1968): op. cit., p. 235.

The prototypical distribution most widely used for stock prices is the lognormal distribution.

4.1.1. Lognormally Distributed Stock Prices

Let $R_T = \frac{S_T}{S_0}$ be the total stock price relative (=return) over T periods of time, where each period has the length τ (e.g. the stock return after T=30 days with 30 periods τ of one day length). If $Y_t = \frac{S_\tau}{S_{\tau-1}}$ is the return from period to period, then R_T is equal to the product of all Y_t: $R_T = \prod_{\tau=1}^{T} Y_\tau$. The natural logarithm of R_T, $\ln R_T$, is the continuously compounded rate of return (CCRR) the stock has offered over the entire time. It is also called its logarithmic return. Considering the T periods,

$$\ln R_T = \ln Y_1 + \ln Y_2 + \ldots\ldots\ldots \ln Y_T$$

i.e. the logarithmic return or CCRR over T periods is just the sum of the CCRR in each period. The successive CCRR's are now assumed to follow a random walk in a fashion that they are independently, but identically distributed. Hence, the CCRR over the entire period, $\ln R_T$, should be normally distributed by the central limit theorem.[106] In particular, if the independently and identically

---

[106] See Ritchken: Options, op. cit., p. 115.

distributed CCRR's per period each have a mean of μ and a variance of σ^2, then the logarithmic return over T periods is normally distributed with mean μT and variance $\sigma^2 T$.

A random variable has a lognormal distribution whenever its logarithm is normally distributed. Hence, the return on the stock R_T is lognormally distributed.[107] Given a particular current stock price S_0, this also implies a lognormal distribution for future stock prices (just multiply $R_T * S_0$). The mean and variance of the distribution are unequivocally related to the mean and variance of the normally distributed logarithm. Most importantly, they are constant. Figure 4.a. shows the shape of the lognormal distribution.

Figure 4.a.: The lognormal distribution

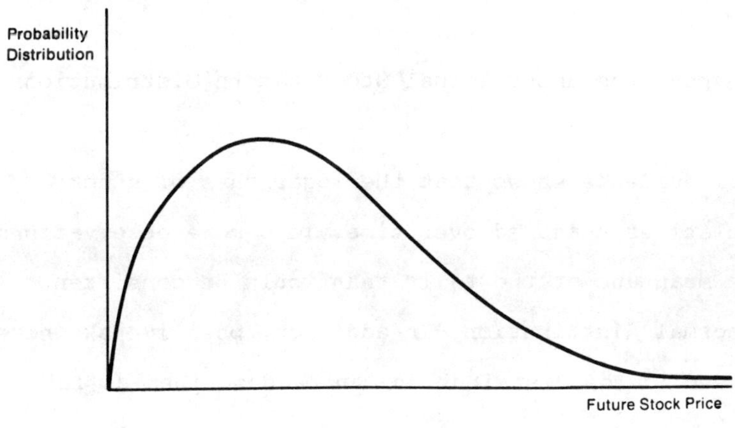

(from: Ritchken, Peter H.: Options: Theory, Strategy and Applications, Glenview, ILL 1987, p.115)

---

[107] See ibid., p. 116.

The lognormal distribution nicely rules out negative values for stock prices and thus has a feature that is very important to capture reality. Black and Scholes assume a particular process that generates stock prices continuously over time. As discussed in Section 3.2., this so-called Brownian motion results in a lognormal stock price distribution at the end of each finite interval, because the logarithmic returns (CCRR) over each tiny time increment are independently, identically and normally distributed. Therefore, any deviations from the normal distribution for logarithmic returns in reality might be a cause for biases in the BS prices. Consequently, we should take a closer look at empirical evidence about the distribution of stock returns in actual markets.

4.1.2. Hypotheses about Actual Stock Return Distributions

Empirical evidence shows that the logarithms of stock price relatives measured over time yield more observations near the mean and at the tails than would be consistent with a normal distribution. In addition, positive skewness is observed.[108] The distribution can be described as fat-

---

[108] See Kon, Stanley J.: Models of stock returns-a comparison, in: JOF 39 (1984), pp. 147-165, here p. 147.

tailed and peaked, also called leptokurtic[109].

An intuitive explanation has been proposed for this finding. For one, a lot of the new information that drives stock prices might be so unrelated that there is little effect on them, thus causing an excessive number of observations around the mean. On the other hand, a small percentage of the news might be so significant that very large changes in the stock price are caused, thus resulting in an excessive number of observations in the tails, compared to the normal distribution.[110]

There are three major hypotheses for a distribution that can capture these deviations from normality. One is the so-called Stable Paretian hypothesis. Its attractive feature is the stability of its parameters, thus making it relatively easy to use in other theoretical concepts where a description of the stock return distribution is needed.[111]

The other two hypotheses postulate a mixture of normal distributions for stock return logarithms in order to explain the observed behavior. If the distribution of return logarithms over successive intervals in calendar

---

[109] See Westerfield, Randolph W.: The distribution of common stock price changes: an application of transactions time and subordinated stochastic models, in: JFQA 12 (1977), pp. 743-765, here p. 743.

[110] See Ritchken: Options, op. cit., p. 118.

[111] See Kon (1984): op. cit., p. 148.

time takes the form of a mixture of normal distributions with different variances but the same mean, fatter tails are the result.[112] Blattberg/Gonedes (1974) show that if the variance is a random variable that follows a so-called inverted gamma distribution, the resulting distribution is student. Using daily stock return data, they compare the performance of this concept with that of the Stable Paretian model and conclude that the student model has greater descriptive validity.[113] If no particular distribution can be assigned to the shift in the variance, the logarithmic stock return distribution can be captured by a discrete mixture of a number of normal distributions. Again, shifts in the variance can explain the fat tails. In addition, shifts in the mean can explain the observed positive skewness.[114]

Kon (1984) conducts an elaborate empirical test on data spanning an 18-year time period. He finds strong evidence that the latter hypothesis best explains the distribution of stock returns logarithms in reality: a discrete mixture of normals.

A comment is appropriate here regarding the effect on the resulting stock price distribution. It was explained

---

[112] See Westerfield (1977): op. cit., p. 747.

[113] See Blattberg, Robert / Gonedes, Nicholas: A comparison of the stable and student distributions as statistical models for stock prices, in: JOB 47 (1974), pp. 244-280, here p. 277.

[114] See Kon (1984): op. cit., p. 160.

above that the terminal stock price distribution will be lognormal if successive logarithmic returns are independently, but <u>identically</u> distributed. The empirical evidence, however, shows that they are <u>not</u> identically distributed. Hence, the terminal stock price distribution will deviate from lognormality, although the particular shape of this deviation is not readily inferable from the leptokurtic shape of the distribution for logarithmic returns.

Intuition and empirical evidence on economic scenarios provide some insight for Kon's finding. Investment and financial decisions by firm managers, macroeconomic variables and institutional trading restrictions should have an impact on the expected return and variance of the stock price. Conducting empirical tests, Beckers (1980) finds an inverse relationship between stock prices and their variance. A significant factor for this relationship is found to be financial leverage, but it cannot entirely explain all the changes in the variance that are observed.[115] Christie (1982), too, finds that the stock price variance increases with financial leverage, again causing the variance to rise when the stock price falls, because leverage rises when the stock price falls.

---

[115] See Beckers, Stan: The constant elasticity of variance model and its implications for option pricing, in: JOF 35 (1980), pp. 661-673, here p. 663-665.

Similarly, increasing operating leverage (fixed costs in relation to the value of the firm) results in increasing variance.[116] The results of Christie's tests show that rising interest rates have the same effect because they raise the required return on the firm (discount factor), thus lowering the market value of the firm. The debt value is found to fall less than the equity value. Thus, leverage rises and consequently the stock price variance rises.[117]

Information signals such as earnings announcements can also result in parameter shifts, in particular leading to increases in the variance around the date of the announcement. This is empirically supported in studies by Beaver (1968) and Patell/Wolfson (1981).[118]

A prominent observation are shifts in the mean and a higher variance for returns from Friday close to Monday close compared to the other days of the week (the "Weekend Effect"). This result supports the notion that more price-relevant information is generated over the weekend than

---

[116] See Christie, Andrew A.: The stochastic behavior of common stock variances, in: JFEC 10 (1982), pp. 407-432, here p. 428.

[117] See ibid. p. 425.
Comment: This is a remarkable result because when viewing stocks as call options on the value of the firm, rising interest rates should raise their price. However, the concurrent decline in the firm value is found to have the dominating influence on the stock price.

[118] See Beaver, William: The information content of annual earnings announcements, in: Empirical Research in Accounting, supplement to the Journal of Accounting Research 6 (1968), pp. 67-92, here p. 81. Also see Patell, James / Wolfson, Mark: The ex ante and ex post price effects of quarterly earnings announcements reflected in option and stock prices, in: Journal of Accounting Research 19 (1981), pp. 434-458, here pp. 447-448.

overnight during the week.[119] Another well-known finding is that mean returns in the first week of January seem to be unusually high (the "January Effect").[120]

Wrapping up these results, stock return logarithms through time appear to switch between a discrete number of normal distributions where one might be a firm-specific information distribution (e.g. leverage), another a macroeconomic distribution (e.g. interest rates), a third a cyclical distribution (e.g. the Weekend Effect) and perhaps some more. There can be parameter shifts to new levels as well as shifts back and forth between particular distributions.[121] Supporting this view, Kon finds that deviations from normality were greatly reduced when looking at yearly subperiods in his sample, which were in turn partitioned by day of the week. The number of distributions per firm is a matter of empirical research and varies across firms (Kon (1984) finds at most four per firm in his sample).[122]

The expected return on the stock is not a variable in the Black-Scholes model. However, the variance is - and it

---

[119] See Kon (1984): op. cit., p. 149.

[120] See Bodie/Kane/Marcus: Investments, op. cit., p. 360.

[121] See Kon (1984): op. cit., p. 152.

[122] See ibid. p. 160.

is assumed to be constant. Yet, the evidence presented here shows that the stock return variance actually changes. The BS model allows an adjustment if σ is a deterministic function of time. In this case, the average σ that will prevail over the life of the option is applicable.[123] However, the evidence above shows that the variance obviously does not display such a simple deterministic behavior.

Further evidence on nonstationary variance and an examination of the biases this causes when BS values are compared to actual market prices will be presented in chapters 7 and 8. Extensions of the BS model that implicitly or explicitly incorporate the variability of the variance as well as empirical evidence on their performance will also be discussed at that point.

4.2. Discrete Trading: Jumps, Circuit Breakers, Legging in and Legging out, and the Resulting Hedging Errors

An obvious feature of real markets that is inconsistent with the BS assumptions is discrete trading. Discrete trading prevents markets from impounding new information into the prices as soon as it becomes available. One example for the results this can have is the Weekend-

---

[123] See Cox/Rubinstein: Options Markets, op. cit., p. 212.

Effect reported above.

More important in the context of option valuation, the accumulation of information overnight or over the weekend can cause prices to jump. This is a serious departure from the Brownian motion assumed for the derivation of the BS model. A related problem is the restriction of minimum price movements on the exchanges (at least one eighth for stocks, at least one sixteenth for options).[124]

A drastic example for jumps was apparent on Oct.19, 1987, the "crash" on Wall Street. On that day, the Dow Jones Industrial Index opened 7 per cent lower than the previous close.[125] One measure conceived to control the market should such a crash occur again was introduced shortly after Black Monday: the so-called circuit breakers. They are maximum daily price movement limits for stocks and futures that trigger the halt of trading if they are reached. Consequently, they are a serious impediment to the price continuity assumption necessary to replicate an option. In fact, they are likely to trap investors in their positions, thus substantially increasing their risk. Once trading resumes, the accumulated impact of previously halted orders may well

---

[124] See Galai (1983): Survey, op. cit., p. 49.

[125] See Rubinstein, Mark: Portfolio insurance and the market crash, in: FAJ (January-February 1988), pp. 38-47, here p. 40.

trigger another large jump.[126]

When jumps occur, it is not possible to appropriately adjust the replicating portfolio in the arbitrage strategy that the BS model employs. Jumps can occur even in continuous markets, where a new price is generated in every infinitely small time increment, if there is a sudden announcement or package of information that causes a large instantaneous price move to a different level. Such a behavior can be modeled by including the possibility of sudden jumps in the stochastic process that describes the stock price movement.[127] Option pricing models that incorporate such jump processes in continuous time will be addressed in Chapter 8.

However, even a continuous time jump process seems unrealistic. Markets are closed overnight and over weekends, and even when they are open, they do not conform to the notion of genuinely continuous trading because they don't generate new prices in every infinitely small time increment. Rather, it takes anywhere from a fraction of a second to several minutes until the next trade occurs. However, the influence this aspect has on errors in hedging is not very large, compared to the trading gaps

---

[126] See ibid. p. 45.

[127] See Merton, Robert C.: Option pricing when the underlying stock returns are discontinuous, in: JFEC 3 (1976), pp. 125-144, here p. 126.

that are caused when the exchange is closed.

Due to discrete trading and the minimum price movement restriction, the stock path looks more like a discrete aggregation of small jumps than a continuous diffusion. This causes hedging errors in the BS replicating portfolio because it cannot be continuously adjusted to continuous, but tiny movements. Hence, an otherwise riskless arbitrage profit on the hedge between the replicating portfolio and the option becomes <u>risky</u>.

Black and Scholes argue in the derivation of their formula that the return on a discretely adjusted option hedge is uncorrelated with the market. Hence, the risk is unsystematic and can be diversified away by holding a large number of hedged positions.[128] Consequently, by regarding unsystematic risk as irrelevant, arbitrage profits should still drive option prices to their BS values because the systematic risk is nil.

However, this line of reasoning is flawed with respect to its actual practicability. Arbitrage profits are defined as sure payoffs from zero investment, thus being totally riskless in terms of systematic <u>and</u> unsystematic risk. Also, the argument of diversifiability of the hedging errors must not be overstretched. It only holds for reasonably small revision intervals, because it

---

[128] See Black/Scholes (1973): op. cit., p. 643.

depends on correlation terms that are virtually zero only for small time increments.[129] They are certainly nonnegligible if one rebalances, say, only once every two months. The requirement to hold a large number of other hedged positions in order to make "riskless" profits on one detected mispricing clearly precludes many of the potential arbitrageurs from taking action.

Discrete trading causes yet another problem. The portfolio adjustment discussed above is regarded to take place simultaneously for every security position that is contained in the hedge. Hence, the prices of the hedge securities cannot get out of line while taking the new positions. However, with discrete trading, this simultaneity is in jeopardy. For example, when the hedge ratio Δ has changed after stock price movements, we might be able to adjust the first leg of our hedge, the position in bonds. But having done this, it is entirely possible that a new trade in the stock, our second leg, does not occur before five minutes have gone by. Until then, the hedge is at risk, because new information can emerge, causing the stock price to move away from the corresponding level that prevailed when the first leg was

[129] See Boyle, Phelim P. / Emanuel, David: Discretely adjusted option hedges, in: JFEC 8 (1980), pp. 259-282, here pp. 276-277.

executed.[130]

Apart from the BS replication, the problem is also apparent in any other arbitrage trade. For example, to take advantage of a put-call parity violation, long and short positions in four securities have to be established. Price movements over the time it takes to execute these four legs generate risk when "legging in". By the time all four trades have finally been carried out, the price changes might have already eliminated the arbitrage opportunity, possibly even turning the established position into a sure loss. Limit orders cannot mitigate the problem because they might result in some legs not being executed at all. When the arbitrage position is terminated, the same difficulties are incurred again while "legging out". Obviously, the problems of legging in and legging out make actual arbitrage activities risky.

4.3. Stochastic Interest Rates

The risk-free interest rate over the life of the option is assumed to be constant in the BS model. However, interest rates do change in reality.

If the interest rate were different in every

---

[130] See Bhattacharya, Mihir: Transactions data tests of Efficiency of the Chicago Board Options Exchange, in: JFEC 12 (1983), pp. 161-185, here pp. 174-175.

instantaneous future period, but known with certainty (deterministic function of time), we would have to associate a different interest rate with every period. It can be shown that under these conditions, the BS model can be corrected by using the average interest rate that will prevail until the option matures.[131] However, interest rates fluctuate randomly, not deterministically, thus making it impossible to carry out such an adjustment.

Merton (1973) has amended the BS model by assuming that interest rates follow a particular stochastic process. Similar to the stock price diffusion process assumed by Black and Scholes, the growth rate in the price of a riskless discount bond maturing at the same date as the option is assumed to follow a Wiener process with certain drift component. However, since the bond price equals its face value at maturity, the variance of this diffusion process is a function of time to maturity.[132] Also, the correlation between the stock price and the bond price has to be recognized. The stochastic bond price has two effects in Merton's approach:

1. The bond and stock price volatility are linked in order to determine a new combined volatility estimate for use in the BS formula.

---

[131] See Cox/Rubinstein: Options Markets, op. cit., p. 212.

[132] See Merton (1973): Theory, op. cit., p. 163.

2. The interest rate to be used in the formula is that paid on the bond with the same maturity as the option.

Since the volatility of the bond price is usually very small compared to that of the stock, the volatility adjustment has little impact on the option value and can therefore usually be omitted. Merton's approach provides theoretical support for dealing with the interest rate problem by using the rate paid on riskless T-bills with the same maturity as the option as an estimate for the interest rate. This has in fact become the common method to determine the interest rate to be used in the BS model.[133]

4.4. Indivisibilities

It is impossible to buy Δ=.7694 shares of stock (for example). When only a small number of options is arbitraged or replicated, the hedge ratio cannot be set to exactly the value that the BS model prescribes.[134] This will of course again induce risk, because the position is over- or under-hedged.

---

[133] See Hull: Options, op. cit., p. 304-305.

[134] See Figlewski, Stephen: Options arbitrage in imperfect markets, in: JOF 44 (1989), pp. 1289-1311, here p. 1298.

Figlewski (1989) examines this problem in a simulation of one-month option hedges that are rebalanced daily. In this simulation, the volatility (risk) of the return from the hedged position is significantly increased when the smallest possible adjustment steps in the hedge ratio are larger than .05.[135]

One might think that indivisibilities cannot be a serious problem in the face of the large positions that are traded by institutional investors and market makers. However, often futures contracts are included in the hedge portfolio in lieu of the stocks, as will be described later in connection with stock index options. This exposes even large positions to the indivisibilities problem, because futures contracts are equivalent to relatively large stock positions. For example, one S&P 500 futures contract controls 500 times the futures price of the Standard & Poors 500 stock index.[136]

---

[135] See ibid. p. 1297.

[136] See Duffie, Darrell: Futures Markets, Englewood Cliffs 1989, p. 140.

4.5. Explicit Transaction Costs: Fees and Commissions

When carrying out trades in securities, explicit transaction costs in the form of fees and commissions are incurred. They are the most obvious obstacle to obtaining arbitrage profits from violations of theoretical pricing relationships, although they are not necessarily the largest one. The fact that most of them are negotiable makes it difficult to assess their exact magnitude.

4.5.1. Trading Structures on the CBOE and the NYSE

The backbone of trading on the Chicago Board Options Exchange (CBOE), the largest options exchange in the United States, are the market makers. Market makers can be individuals with an own seat on the CBOE, but most are employees of specialized firms and brokerage houses that have bought seats on the exchange. For each option, numerous market makers compete in an open outcry auction system. They take the opposite side of public orders and provide liquidity by risking their own capital.[137] Floor brokers, the second group of traders on the CBOE, only act as agents for public orders and hence cannot engage in

---

[137] See Chicago Board Options Exchange: Fundamental facts about the world's largest options marketplace.

arbitrage.[138]

On the New York Stock Exchange (NYSE), the specialist is the central figure in the execution of trades. Each specialist makes the market in one or more shares.[139] However, stock exchange specialists are not permitted to trade in futures or options on stocks for which they make a market and are thus excluded from options arbitrage trades.[140] But the traders and arbitrageurs with a seat on the stock exchange that trade with the specialists don't have that restriction and are thus candidates for options arbitrage trades that involve positions in the underlying stocks.

4.5.2. Floor Trading and Clearing Fees

Option market makers have to pay floor trading and clearing fees, which are charged by the exchange, the clearing corporation and the clearing firms on a per-contract basis for handling the transaction.[141] Clearing is the recognition of the transaction by the Options

---

[138] Some other options marketplaces employ a specialist system similar to that on the New York Stock Exchange, but due to its dominant position, the CBOE and its trading structure is the relevant benchmark.

[139] See Bodie/Kane/Marcus: Investments, op. cit., p. 83.

[140] See Phillips, Susan M. / Smith, Clifford W.: Trading costs for listed options, in: JFEC 8 (1980), pp. 179-201, here p. 180.

[141] See Chance, Don M.: An Introduction to Options and Futures, Chicago 1989, p. 47.

Clearing Corporation (OCC) and constitutes the actual cash settlement of the trade. Since the capital requirements for membership in the OCC are fairly stringent, many market makers on the CBOE clear through a few clearing firms that are a member of the OCC. These firms also provide additional services such as bookkeeping, regulatory comliance and financial information.[142]

The clearing business is highly competitive, and thus the fees charged by the clearing firms are generally lower for market makers with high trading volumes. Phillips and Smith (1980) estimate between \$.50 and \$1 per option contract (which covers 100 shares), while Bhattacharya (1983) states \$.36 for high volume option market makers.

The lower limit on these fees is of course determined by the fees the clearing firms themselves as OCC members are charged. These bounds are also the relevant figures for the few market makers that are members of the OCC and hence don't have to clear through a clearing firm. The OCC charges its members \$0.075 per option contract.[143] In addition, the CBOE charges exchange fees of \$0.30 per option contract (on 100 shares) if the option costs over \$1 (per share), and \$0.15 if the option costs less than \$1. For index options, the exchange fees are \$0.40 and

---

[142] See Phillips/Smith (1980): op. cit., p. 195.

[143] See Cox/Rubinstein: Options Markets, op. cit., p. 70.

$0.20, respectively.[144]

An additional function of the OCC is to randomly select an option writer among its members to deliver the shares (in the case of a call) or the striking price (in the case of a put) when an option is exercised. For each exercise notice tendered, the OCC charges $1 to the selected OCC member (clearing firm), which in turn assigns the notice to one of its market making customers.[145] (Finally, the exercise notice reaches a private investor at the end of the financial intermediation chain.)

According to Phillips and Smith (1980), floor commission rates for traders with a seat on the NYSE range from $1 to $4 per round lot of 100 shares, with an average around $2. Again, the exact size of the fees is dependent upon the trading volume.

Option market makers are usually not simultaneously members of the NYSE or some other exchange.[146] Therefore, they must act as customers of stock exchange members to conduct options arbitrage strategies that require positions in stocks. For sufficiently large volumes, Bhattacharya (1983) estimates the commissions for the correspondent on the stock exchange to be around $4.50 per

---

[144] See Chicago Board Options Exchange: Fee Schedule as of July 1, 1989.

[145] See Cox/Rubinstein: Options Markets, op. cit., pp. 70-71.

[146] See Phillips/Smith (1980): op. cit., p. 197.

round lot of stocks. Conversely, an arbitrageur who is a member of a stock exchange might pay fees as low as $1 per round lot, but has to pay $.80 per option contract because he has to trade with a market maker on the options exchange.[147]

The exact level of the fees stated in the above mentioned academic literature is volume dependent, subject to change, and might be somewhat outdated[148]. Nonetheless, this does not in any way impede the illustration of the main point to be made by their presentation: in terms of transaction costs, members of the stock exchange and market makers on the options exchange are the most advantageously placed traders.[149] Any other investor has to go through - and pay - more intermediaries. When it comes to assessing whether an arbitrage trade is profitable after transaction costs, these two groups are the benchmark. In particular, the option market maker is the most advantageously placed trader for arbitrage in option positions alone (e.g. the box spread).

---

[147] See Bhattacharya (1983): op. cit., p. 167.

[148] More recent estimates in academic articles that use these fees to conduct empirical tests could not be found.

[149] See Bhattacharya (1983): op. cit., p. 167.

4.5.3. Brokerage Commissions

For investments in options and stocks, brokerage firms are the intermediaries for the general public. The larger retail brokerage firms are usually members of stock or options exchanges, i.e. they do not themselves need yet another intermediary to reach the trading floor.[150] Discount brokerage houses give little investment advice, but offer lower commissions in return. Full service brokers are more expensive.[151] Again, the volume and size of the transaction has a substantial impact on the charged brokerage commission.

Some large institutional investors can negotiate very low commission rates with their brokers. However, their overall transaction costs can never be lower than those incurred by option market makers or stock exchange members, because those don't pay any brokerage commissions at all for trades on their respective exchange.

The individual, personal investor whose trading volume is too small to give him any negotiating power incurs the highest commissions. There is usually a fixed charge, combined with some additional percentage rate that depends

---

[150] See Phillips/Smith (1980): op. cit. p. 180.

[151] See Chance: Introduction, op. cit., p. 49.

on the size of the transaction.[152] Below, option and stock commissions charged by Fidelity Investments are given as an example:

Fidelity Investments

ALL STOCKS

Transaction	Commission Rate
$ 0 – 2,500	$ 25.75 + 1.6% of principal
$ 2,501 – 6,000	$ 50.75 + .6% of principal
$ 6,001 – 22,000	$ 68.75 + .3% of principal
$ 22,001 – 50,000	$ 90.75 + .2% of principal
$ 50,001 – 500,000	$140.75 + .1% of principal
$500,001 +	$240.75 + .08% of principal

Minimum Charge: $.085 per share on the first 1,000 shares, plus $.04 per share thereafter. (Not to exceed maximum charge).

Maximum Charge: $48 for the first 100 shares, plus $.49 per share thereafter; or one-half of principal amount (whichever is less).

All stock transactions are subject to an overriding minimum of $36.

OPTIONS

Transaction	Commission Rate
$ 0 – 2,500	$28.75 + 1.6% of principal
$ 2,501 – 10,000	$48.75 + .8% of principal
$ 10,001 +	$98.75 + .3% of principal

Minimum Charge: $34.25 plus $1.75 per contract (Not to exceed maximum charge).

Maximum Charge: $36 per contract for the first two contracts, plus $4 per contract thereafter; or one-half of principal amount (whichever is less).

All option transactions are subject to an overriding minimum of $36.

Commissions on options transactions are charged when options are bought or sold (written) and when they are exercised.[153] When exercising a stock option, the investor must also pay the stock commission. This cost is not incurred when exercising a cash settlement option, for example the S+P 100 stock index option. Also, no commission is charged when an option expires.[154]

---

[152] See ibid. p. 49.

[153] See Marshall, John F.: Futures and Option Contracting, Cincinnati 1989, p. 34.

[154] See Chance: Introduction, op. cit., p. 49.

4.6. The Bid-Ask Spread: an Implicit Transaction Cost

The bid-ask spread is the difference between the highest bid to buy and the lowest offer to sell. Market makers on the CBOE and specialists on the stock exchange perform the function of providing liquidity. They permanently quote a higher price at which they are willing to sell and a lower price at which they are willing to buy. The fraction of a point they make on the bid-ask spread is their income for providing liquidity service.[155]

4.6.1. Who Incurs the Bid-Ask Spread?

Obviously, any public investor incurs the expense of the bid-ask spread. In the context of options arbitrage trades that involve stock positions, the spread in the stock market is unavoidable even for exchange members. As mentioned above, the only ones who might get around it - the specialists - are not allowed to trade options on the stocks in which they make a market.

At first glance, one might think that the market makers on the options exchange are exempt from the spread on option prices. However, this is not true. For a market maker to actively establish a position, he must often

---

[155] See ibid. p. 50.

trade with a competing market maker.[156] Otherwise, he might forego the arbitrage opportunity while waiting for a public sell order to come up at his bid price. If the position is prematurely closed at a later date (i.e. the market maker realizes his arbitrage profit early when prices have moved back in line instead of waiting until expiration), the market maker will likely only get another market maker's bid price. Hence, he incurs half the bid-ask spread again (if one assumes that the true option price lies at the midpoint of the spread).[157]

4.6.2. Estimation of the Bid-Ask Spread Costs

Not all transactions occur at the stated bid or ask price. Phillips and Smith (1980) report that over 40 per cent of the trades occur inside the spread that is quoted at any particular point in time. This can happen, for example, when floor brokers execute public orders, thereby offering more attractive prices to the traders and thus also to a market maker who wants to open or close an arbitrage position. Trades inside the spread are one aspect that makes it difficult to assess the exact cost arising from it.

---

[156] See Phillips/Smith (1980): op. cit., p. 183.

[157] See ibid. p. 187.

In addition, the percentage spread is not uniform across options, but depends on several factors. When providing liquidity service, the market maker faces price uncertainty for his inventory position as well as arrival uncertainty because he does not know when somebody will react to his quotes and trade with him.[158] Obviously, this uncertainty will be higher the thinner the market, i.e. the less transactions occur. Therefore, spreads on options with high volume tend to be lower.[159] The same line of reasoning applies to stocks.

Another factor influencing the bid-ask spread is the relation of an option's price to the sensitivity it shows regarding changes in variables. It can be easily shown that the volatility of an option equals its elasticity times the underlying stock's σ.[160] The option elasticity is $\frac{\partial C}{\partial S}\frac{S}{C}=\Delta_C\frac{S}{C}$ for calls and $\frac{\partial P}{\partial S}\frac{S}{P}=\Delta_P\frac{S}{P}$ for puts. It rises the further the option gets out-of-the-money, reflecting the increasing leverage in the replicating portfolio.[161] Options are consequently a riskier inventory position the further out-of-the-money they are. Accordingly, higher

---

[158] See Ho, Thomas S. / Macris, Richard G.: Dealer bid-ask quotes and transaction prices: an empirical study of some AMEX options, in: JOF 39 (1984), pp. 23-45, here p. 27.

[159] See Phillips/Smith: op. cit., p. 183.

[160] See Cox/Rubinstein: Options Markets, op. cit., pp. 186-188.

[161] See ibid. pp. 228-229 and p. 235.

percentage bid-ask spreads are found.[162] On the other hand, changes in σ have the greatest impact when the option is at-the-money.

Finally, there is the factor of information trading. One function of the spread is to protect the market maker from losses when he trades with somebody who has new information.[163] When disseminated, new information will change the option price through changes in the variables that influence it. Since investors can get more percentage movement on options than on stocks (because of the levered character of options), many investors will prefer to trade options instead of stocks when they feel they have new information that is not yet incorporated in the prices. With respect to information trading, the environment for options market makers may be riskier than in the stock market.

Percentage spreads for stocks are generally lower than for options. For example, Phillips and Smith (1980) found an average bid-ask spread 4.5 per cent for calls and 5.9 per cent for puts in their sample, while the spread on the underlying stocks was less than one per cent.

However, the main point to be reiterated here is that

---

[162] See Ho/Macris (1984): op. cit., p. 37.

[163] See Black (1975): op. cit., p. 61.

no market participant who can engage in options arbitrage trades can entirely avoid the bid-ask spread.

A second type of implicit transaction costs that plays a major role in the markets are the so-called market impact costs. They can arise when large positions are bought or sold. The discussion of market impact costs is deferred to subsection 4.9.2., because they are most obvious in the context of portfolio insurance.

4.7. Restrictions to Short Sales

With respect to option valuation, restrictions regarding short sales are of interest because the arbitrage relationships and pricing frameworks involve short positions in stocks and options. When stocks are sold short, the investor must borrow them from another investor through a broker. The proceeds from the short sale, however, are not paid out. They are kept in a noninterest bearing account.[164] This causes costs because the arbitrageur might now have to borrow additional money to establish his position without getting any compensation for the interest he pays on the loan. If the arbitrageur does have sufficient funds, he incurs opportunity costs

[164] See Cox/Rubinstein: Options Markets, op. cit., p. 103.

because he cannot lend and earn interest on them.

In addition, the investor has to put up a margin that serves as collateral against losses from the short position if the stock price moves up. Regulation T of the Federal Reserve Act authorizes the Federal Reserve to regulate credit extension in the United States. This authority also encompasses margin credit on stocks and options. The NYSE and the options exchanges also have set up rules that determine the minimum initial and maintenance margins on stock and option transactions.[165] The <u>initial margin</u> is the minimum amount in per cent of the position value an investor has to supply on the day of the transaction. The minimum <u>maintenance margin</u> determines the amount of funds required on balance each day thereafter.[166]

For stock short sales, the minimum initial margin is fifty per cent.[167] If the stock price rises, the unrealized losses on the short position are (hypothetically) subtracted from the margin to cover the gap. The minimum maintenance margin is 25 per cent of the current value of the short position. If after subtracting the gap, the margin falls below this level, additional

---

165 See Cox/Rubinstein: Options Markets, op. cit., p. 98.

166 See Chance: Introduction, op. cit., p. 56.

167 See ibid. p. 56.

money has to be put up or the position will be closed.

Margin can be put up in the form of interest earning securities such as T-bills.[168] Thus, in contrast to the unusable short sale proceeds, margin requirements do not cause any economic loss to an investor who has sufficient capital.

Shorting a call means writing a call without owning the underlying shares. Shorting a put means writing a put without reserving the money to pay the striking price in case it is exercised against the investor. Such positions are called "uncovered" or "naked". Uncovered positions require a margin of 30 per cent (both initial and maintenance) of the stock price, plus the in-the-money amount (because it is an additional obligation to the writer) or less the out-of-the-money amount.[169]

As the stock price moves, the margin is adjusted accordingly, thus requiring additional money to cover gaps or freeing up money when the stock moves in a favorable direction. For more complicated positions like spreads and combinations, more complicated margin rules apply. However, the main point to note is that the restrictions for uncovered option positions never generate an economic loss. The margin can be put up in form of interest bearing

---

[168] See Bodie/Kane/Marcus: Investments, op. cit., p. 89.

[169] See Cox/Rubinstein: Options Markets, op. cit., p. 104.

T-bills, and in contrast to shorting stocks, the option writer does get the proceeds from the short sale.[170]

To summarize, margin requirements for shorted stocks or options don't cause additional costs because interest is earned on them. The problem is that the proceeds from stock short sales cannot be used by the investor. However, this factor may not always be relevant. Many large investors engaging in large arbitrage and replication strategies hold considerable inventories of various stocks. For them, a stock short sale might well be implemented by reducing a long position.[171]

This also circumvents the final short sale restriction to be mentioned here: the uptick rule. Short sales are only permitted after an upward price movement in order to prevent waves of speculation. Unless the investor or market maker has an inventory in the stocks or options to be sold, this can cause delays and hence increase the risks in legging in and legging out.[172]

Under normal market conditions, the short sale restrictions should not have any major impact on options arbitrage and the valuation frameworks based on it. However, under extreme conditions like the crash of '87,

---

[170] See ibid. p. 64.

[171] See Thorp, Edward: Extensions of the Black-Scholes option model, in: Proceedings of the 39th Session of the International Statistical Institute, Vienna, Austria (August 1973).

[172] See Phillips/Smith (1980): op. cit., p. 198.

pressures to put up more margin and long delays due to the uptick rule may well cause problems.

4.8. Taxation of Option Transactions

The Tax Reform Act of 1986 abolished the former distinction between the tax rates for long and short term capital gains. All capital gains income is taxed at the taxpayer's ordinary income rate. Equivalently, losses are deductible against the investor's income, thus lowering his tax burden.[173]

Here is a brief overview of the taxation of option transactions:[174]

a) Long calls:

The profit on a long call position that is sold back at a later date is taxed at the ordinary income rate. Losses from sale at a lower price or worthless expiration are deductible accordingly. However, if the call is exercised, the original call price plus the striking price is viewed as the stock's purchase price. This purchase price is used to determine a future capital gain or loss on the stock, but a tax liability or deduction does not arise before the

[173] See Marshall, John F.: Futures and Option Contracting, Cincinnati 1989, p. 612.

[174] See Chance: Introduction, op. cit., pp. 58-60.

stock is sold.

b) Short (written) calls:

If an investor sells a call and later buys it back, or if it expires, gains are taxable at the ordinary rate and losses are deductible. If the call is exercised against the writer, the original call price plus the exercise price is viewed as the stock's sale price.

c) Long puts:

Profits and losses on a long put that is sold at a later date or expires are taxed at the ordinary income rate or deductible, respectively. If the investor exercises the put, the exercise price minus the original put price he paid is viewed as the stock's sale price. The profit from the stock sale is then taxed at the ordinary income rate. Alternatively, the investor can use the exercise of the put to sell short the stock, thus deferring any realization and taxation of a gain until the short position in the stock is closed.

d) Short (written) puts:

When bought back before maturity or if it expires, gains or losses on a written put are taxed at the ordinary rate or deductible, respectively. If the put is exercised against the writer, the striking price minus the original put price is viewed as the stock's purchase price and used to determine gains or losses on the stock.

e) Index options:

Index options have a special tax status because at year's end, all realized and unrealized gains or losses on them are taxed.

An interesting aspect to taxation is the strategy of using options in order to defer taxation of capital gains into the next calendar year or even indefinitely. There are several ways to do this. One is to simply buy a protective put in order to "insure" an unrealized capital gain on a long stock position.[175] Another tax deferral strategy is to exercise long option positions. By exercising a profitable long call position, taxation of the gain can be deferred indefinitely until the stock is sold. The same is true for profitable long put positions if they are exercised by selling short the stock.

Although tax deferral might conceivably influence option trading, a different consideration is of much greater interest for option valuation:[176] If the writer of a call owns the underlying stock and does not plan to sell it, he won't realize any gains or losses on it. On the other hand, any gains he realizes on the call when it

---

[175] See Marshall: Futures, op. cit., p. 611.

[176] See Scholes, Myron: Taxes and the pricing of options, in: JOF 31 (1976), pp. 319-322, here pp. 322-323.

expires or when he buys it back at a lower price will be taxed. Equivalently, any losses are deductible if the writer buys the option back at a higher price; or, if he buys additional stock to deliver at the lower striking price when the call is exercised. Effectively, this combination of a "non-taxed" stock position with the regular taxation of the call alters the after tax hedge ratio a covered writer faces because the government assumes part of the risk.[177]

On the other hand, market makers and dealers usually don't hold long-term stock positions on which they write calls. They buy and sell stocks and options all the time while performing their function as providers of liquidity and intermediation. Therefore, their gains and losses on both stocks and options are realized and taxed, thus mutually canceling out the effect on the hedge ratio. In fact, dealers and market makers are in the same situation as tax exempt investors such as pension funds. For them, taxation has no influence on the valuation of the call. The same effects apply to puts.[178]

A more detailed examination of this disparity in the taxation of market participants will be presented in Chapter 8 because it can explain biases that have been

---

[177]See Black (1975): op. cit., p. 62.

[178]See Scholes (1976): op. cit., pp. 320 and 324.

found when comparing BS values to market prices.

4.9. Limited Choices and Information Effects

Several obstacles that keep markets from operating according to investors' needs must be mentioned. They might appear subtle at first glance but can have a significant impact in certain situations.

4.9.1. Option Availability, Maturity, and Position Limits

A serious impediment to the development of an efficient option market are the position limits. They were conceived in order to prevent one investor from controlling the market. In CBOE stock options, they range from 3000 to 8000 contracts (each covering 100 options), while the maximum position in index options is limited to 25,000 contracts.[179] The position limits are the reason why options are not very widely used by institutional investors. Therefore, trading volume is kept on lower levels than it could be. However, this is unfortunate because trading volume has been shown to be an important

---

[179] See Chicago Board Options Exchange: Fundamental Facts about the World's Largest Options Marketplace

factor in improving pricing efficiency.[180]

Options are not available for every stock. The CBOE lists options on 178 widely traded stocks. However, investors who want to purchase stock options that are not traded on any options exchange are forced to replicate them. Moreover, options are only available for maturities up to nine months, and they are only issued for striking prices close to the current stock price.[181] An investor who wants to purchase an option with a longer maturity or an unavailable striking price is again forced to replicate it.

Position limits and the unavailability of options impede the conveyance of information about dynamic hedging strategies and hence raise stock volatility, as shown below.

4.9.2. Portfolio Insurance, Information Conveyance, and Market Impact Costs

A means for circumventing the unavailability of a desired option or the limitation to a particular position size is to simply replicate the option with the Black-Scholes

---

[180] See Gastineau, Gary L.: The time has come to eliminate option position limits, in: FAJ (July-August 1988) pp. 7-8, here p. 8.

[181] See Chicago Board Options Exchange: Fundamental Facts about the World's Largest Options Marketplace.

dynamic hedging strategy. A prominent example for this is portfolio insurance (PI). Portfolio insurers protect the value of large portfolios by employing protective put positions.[182] Frequently, traded puts are unavailable for the securities contained in the portfolio. In other cases, they can't be acquired in the necessary quantities because of position limits, or the desired striking price or maturity is unavailable. For example, the time horizon for many PI programs is several years. Therefore, the put is replicated by selling off stock according to the put's Δ and by investing an appropriate amount in T-bills.[183]

However, there will be an impact on the price of the underlying stock when large orders that originate from PI are added to the anticipated "typical" order flow.[184] Sell orders arise when the stock price falls because the falling Δ of the put requires to sell off or short more stock. Traders and speculators who did not have any information to prepare for this will buy additional supply only at a discount. This discount reflects the risk they will carry until the additional inventory can be reduced in the future.[185] The rationale also applies in the other

---

[182] See Bodie/Kane/Marcus: Investments, op. cit., p. 601.

[183] Often, index futures are employed in the replicating portfolio instead of the stocks themselves, as will be shown in Section 4.11.

[184] See Duffie: Futures Markets, op. cit., p. 145.

[185] See ibid. p. 145.

direction. When portfolio insurers have large buy orders after the stock price has risen, they will get the stocks only at a premium.

This effect is called a market impact cost. It is an implicit transaction cost the portfolio insurer or any other investor incurs when he sells or buys large positions. These orders in effect drive the stock price away from where it would be according to fundamental information.[186] Market impact costs are thus a form of market imperfection.

Since the market impact is a deviation from fundamentals, an investor who buys at the "too low" market impact prices caused by PI sales has a higher expected return from the position than prescribed by the fundamental data.[187] Taking positions to profit from this is called market timing. However, there is not unlimited capital available to engage in market timing activities when the impact occurs. For most investors, it is costly to shift assets to the market timing activity on short notice, even though it is a profitable opportunity. For example, pension funds invest a major part of their capital in mortgages or physical structures. Other asset

---

[186] See Grossman, Sanford J.: An analysis of the implications for stock and future price volatility of program trading and dynamic hedging strategies, in: JOB 61 (1988), pp. 275-298, here p. 287.

[187] See ibid. p. 281.

managers must adhere to a fixed composition of their portfolio. It is impossible to free up this capital from one minute to the next.[188] This capital constraint is the reason why the market impact occurs in the first place. In the absence of information about possible future PI activity, only an "average" amount of capital which is adequate for the "average situation" is committed to market timing.[189]

In a market where an option on the stock is traded, and where there are no position limits for its use for PI (thus making replication unnecessary), the market impact cost will initially show up in a rising put price. The put price will rise because the stock price deviations caused by the market impact in effect raise the stock's volatility. Portfolio insurers who have a choice between dynamic replication and buying a traded put will buy the put until its price reflects that additional volatility.[190] But this price also conveys the information about PI to traders and speculators who can commit capital to market timing activity. The higher put price signals the higher expected return from committing capital to profit from the market impact. Speculators will

---

[188] See ibid. p. 280.

[189] See ibid. p. 290.

[190] See ibid. p. 288.

hence in advance set aside a larger amount of capital to profit from future market impacts when they observe the higher put price.

However, this higher level of committed capital will reduce the future volatility and market impact. This leads to an important conclusion. The volatility can be substantially lower when options are traded on the stock, and when there are no restrictions on the options' use.[191] Empirical evidence confirms that stock price volatility has fallen after options on the stock were introduced.[192] Even if markets are complete and if there are no transaction costs, the above discussion shows that the replication argument does not make traded options redundant because they are not informationally redundant.

The discussion above shows that the Black-Scholes dynamic replication strategy may not work if there are impediments to arbitraging a traded option with the replicating portfolio. The BS model implicitly relies on the assumption that the underlying stock price is independent of the number of investors who engage in the replicating strategy. However, if the synthetic portfolio

---

[191] See ibid. p. 288.

[192] See Hayes, Samuel L. / Tennenbaum, Michael E.: The impact of listed options on the underlying shares, in: FM 8 (1979), pp. 72-77, here p. 72.

cannot be arbitraged as desired with a traded option, e.g. because of position limits, this assumption clearly does not hold: due to insufficient information conveyance, there won't be sufficient capital available to prevent prices from jumping when all the synthetic positions are simultaneously adjusted after price moves.[193] The market impact exacerbates the discontinuous trading that was discussed earlier in this chapter. It is inconsistent with the assumptions that have to hold in order to value options with the BS formula.

A drastic demonstration of market impact costs was the stock market crash in Oct. '87. Although the exact cause of the crash is disputed, the failure of attempts to implement PI on Oct. 19 was apparent. The existing price discontinuity in the market on that day was already an impediment to PI with synthetic positions. But it was exacerbated by high market impact costs, which reached estimated levels of up to one per cent.[194]

An interesting proposal to mitigate these problems is the so-called <u>sunshine trading</u>, where portfolio insurers announce their planned action some time in advance, thus allowing traders and speculators to commit adequate

---

[193] See Grossman (1988): op. cit., p. 277.

[194] See Rubinstein, Mark: Portfolio insurance and the market crash, in: FAJ (January/February 1988), pp. 38-47, here p. 39.

capital.[195]

Attempts to systematically quantify market impact costs or to incorporate them as a separate component in valuation models have not yet been made. Nevertheless, it is important to recognize their effects.

4.10. Different Borrowing and Lending Rates and their Combination with Transaction Costs

Gilster and Lee (1984) study the case of different borrowing and lending rates. Borrowing can be replicated by shorting stock and buying $1/\Delta_C$ calls per share shorted. (Equivalently, one can short Δ_C shares for each call long.) This is called a borrowing hedge. It creates an immediate cash inflow that should cost the borrowing rate until the position is closed at expiration. Lending can be replicated by buying stock and writing $1/\Delta_C$ calls per share long. This is called an investment hedge because it requires an initial cash outlay that should earn the risk free rate of return. The hedges are rebalanced appropriately.

If the borrowing rate is higher than the lending rate, the call price in the borrowing hedge (C_B) must be higher than the call price in the investment hedge (C_L) because

---

[195] See ibid. p. 43.

call option prices rise when the interest rate rises. Intuitively, this looks like an arbitrage opportunity. If the market price C lies between C_L and C_B, lenders could try to write calls at C (which is $>C_L$), while borrowers could try to buy them at C (which is $<C_B$). However, the introduction of transaction costs complicates the picture.

When transaction costs from initiating and rebalancing the hedges are considered, the appropriate borrowing hedge call price C_B that the borrower has to pay must be lowered in order to compensate for them. Likewise, the appropriate lending hedge call price C_L that the lender receives when writing it must be raised in order to still provide the lender with the risk free lending rate net of transaction costs.[196]

Using Brownian motion for the stock price, Gilster and Lee simulate this effect. They consider transaction costs that are proportional (fixed percentage rate) to the value of the stocks and options bought and sold when initiating and rebalancing the hedges. Transaction costs of 2% for options and 1.25% for stocks are assumed. However, the analysis employs adding on expected transaction costs until option maturity, which ignores the fact that the necessary amount of rebalancing is totally uncertain

---

[196] See Gilster, John E. / Lee, William: The effects of transaction costs and different borrowing and lending rates on the option pricing model: a note, in: JOF 39 (1984), pp. 1215-1221, here p. 1216.

because it depends on the movement of the stock. The hedge ratio changes most when the stock price moves around the striking price, while an option that has moved into the money or out of the money requires far less rebalancing and hence less transaction costs. Transaction costs are stock path dependent and hence correlated with the market.[197] If one rebalances continuously, the transaction costs will approach infinity. Therefore, the argument that discretely adjusted hedge returns are uncorrelated with the market is employed to justify daily rebalancing in the simulation. In this context, it is interesting to note that holding the stock position constant and instead adjusting the number of options held or written is the favored strategy. Rebalancing the option position involves much smaller dollar amounts and hence smaller transaction costs.[198]

Three different outcomes are possible:[199]
In the first case, the rebalancing produces transaction costs that raise the appropriate lending hedge call price and lower the appropriate borrowing call price so much that C_L ends up <u>above</u> C_B. This creates a range between C_L

---

[197] See Leland, Hayne E.: Option pricing and replication with transactions costs, in: JOF 40 (1985), pp. 1283-1301, here p. 1289.

[198] See Gilster/Lee (1984): op. cit., p. 1217. Comment: It should be noted, however, that adjustment of the option position causes more problems with respect to indivisibilities, because each option contract covers 100 shares.

[199] See ibid. p. 1220.

and C_B in which borrowing as well as investment hedges are less attractive than borrowing or investing directly, respectively. Arbitrage should keep the option price within this range, but a precise price for the option cannot be determined.

In the second case, transaction costs raise C_L and lower C_B by an amount that lets them precisely coincide, i.e. $C_L=C_B$. Here, the effect of differing borrowing and lending rates is canceled by the transaction costs, thus yielding a unique option price.

In the third case, the transaction costs are insufficient to raise C_L above C_B. Consequently, there is again a range within which the option price is kept. However, in this case the arbitrage opportunity with direct borrowing or lending that was mentioned above prevails. In fact, this range constitutes a stable disequilibrium in which the option simultaneously offers a higher rate of return on the investment hedge than lending directly (e.g. by buying T-bills) and a lower borrowing rate on the borrowing hedge than direct borrowing would cost. In this situation, options would provide society's lowest cost form of financial intermediation.[200]

Given a particular interest rate gap and the assumed transaction costs, it is shown that reaching one of the

---

[200]See ibid. p. 1217.

three cases above depends on the stock volatility as well as the time to expiration and the striking price. Yet, the only systematic result that can be stated is that case 1 is more probable the smaller the gap between the borrowing and lending rates and the higher the transaction costs.

If the disequilibrium of the third case were common in reality, it should prompt huge arbitrage activities to ultimately drive the gap between borrowing and lending rates to a level where case 2 or case 1 is reached. Gilster and Lee's simulation does not rule out this somewhat disturbing situation. However, it should be recalled that apart from the assumed level of proportional transaction costs, none of the other factors and market imperfections discussed so far are incorporated in the analysis (e.g. deviations from Brownian motion). The questionable simplification to ignore the path dependency of transaction costs was already addressed above. If the additional effect of these factors raised the total measure of incurred transaction costs, case 3 would become less likely. Hence, more complex studies are necessary to find out whether case 3 does actually occur in reality.

While this question remains unanswered, the theoretical relationship that arises when combining different borrowing and lending rates with transaction costs is an interesting result and should be kept in mind.

4.11. Special Considerations for Index Options

Stock index options are options on an imaginary portfolio of stocks that duplicates the composition of a stock market index. Currently, the most popular index option is the OEX 100, which is traded on the CBOE. It is an option on the Standard & Poor's 100 stock index.[201] In contrast to stock options, index options cannot be exercised in the literal sense where the underlying shares are delivered. They are always settled in form of a cash payment equivalent to the difference between the striking price and the index value at the close of the exercise date.[202]

A real-world problem is the virtual impossibility to replicate an index option. This would require constant readjustment within a stock portfolio containing weighted[203] proportions of the component stocks, as well as rebalancing of the position held in this entire portfolio according to the hedge ratio.

This problem can be avoided by using index futures. These considerations are also important in the context of

---

201 See Chicago Board Options Exchange: Fundamental Facts about the World's Largest Options Marketplace.

202 See Chicago Board Options Exchange: S&P 100 Index Options: the Index Edge, Chicago 1988, p. 8.

203 The S&P 100 and S&P 500 stock indices are market value-weighted. The same is true for other broadly based indices such as the Wilshire 5000 index. In contrast, the Dow Jones Industrial Average is a price-weighted index, where the weight of each firm is proportional to its share price rather than to the outstanding market value of the shares. See Bodie/Kane/Marcus: Investments, op. cit., pp. 60-65.

portfolio insurance.

4.11.1. The Spot-Futures Parity

Arbitrage provides that the spread between the spot price and the current futures price (which is payable at some future date) is determined by a fixed relationship. This relationship, assuming constant interest rates, can be derived in the following manner:[204]

	cash flow today	cash flow at time T
Portfolio 1: buy stock	$-S_0$	S_T
Portfolio 2: long futures	0	S_T-F_0
invest F_0e^{-rt} in T-bills	$-F_0e^{-rt}$	F_0

where the subscripts 0 and T denote today and the expiration date of the futures contract, respectively, and t is the time to the maturity date T. F_0 is the current futures price for a contract maturing at time T (i.e. the buyer of the contract has to buy the underlying security at the price of F_0 when the contract matures at time T). The cash flow at time T is equal for both strategies. Therefore, to rule out arbitrage, the two portfolios must cost the same. Hence:

---

[204] See Bodie/Kane/Marcus: Investments, op. cit., p. 642.

$F_0e^{-rt} = S_0$ or equivalently $F_0 = S_0e^{rt}$

Explained intuitively, the futures contract makes it possible to purchase an asset at some delivery date T in the future at a certain, fixed price F_0. Consequently, the interest that can be earned in the meantime on the funds that would be needed to purchase the asset right away is the "cost" for delaying the purchase, thus raising the futures price above the spot price. At delivery date T (with t=0), the futures price F_t must equal the spot price.

4.11.2. Using Index Futures to Replicate an Index Option

It follows from the spot-futures parity that futures contracts on the index can easily be used instead of the underlying stocks in order to replicate the index option. If the option's hedge ratio prescribes to hold or short Δ "shares" of the underlying index, one can alternatively use Δe^{-rt} futures instead.[205] Note that this strategy requires additional continuous adjustment of the futures position as time passes by (t declines), even if the hedge ratio does not change.

In addition to easier replication, futures contracts

---

[205] This is not exactly feasible in practice. As mentioned before, one futures contract covers several hundred times the index value, thus giving rise to the indivisibility problem when employed in dynamic replication.

also provide an advantage in terms of transaction costs. They have been estimated to be around one tenth of those incurred on the underlying stocks.[206] This advantage is not available for single stocks because futures contracts on single stocks are not traded in the United States.[207]

4.11.3. Problems in the Use of Futures and their Implications for Portfolio insurance

Although the spot-futures parity seems to be a tight relationship, transaction costs can drive futures prices away from it, thus causing inaccuracies when the portfolio is rebalanced. The same effect occurs when investors with new information trade in the futures market first because the transaction costs there are lower. This causes futures prices to "lead" the stock market, i.e. it takes a while until stock index arbitrageurs restore the spot-futures parity.[208]

A related problem arises because the stocks in the index are not traded continuously. Hence, some of the stock prices that are used to compute the reported current

---

[206]See Figlewski (1989): op. cit., p. 1308.

[207]See Bodie/Kane/Marcus: Investments, op. cit., p. 630.

[208]See Siegel, Daniel R. / Siegel, Diane F.: Futures Markets, Orlando, FL 1990, p. 88.

index value can be several minutes old. This creates uncertainty regarding the fair value of the index futures because the reported price of the underlying index does not entirely correspond to current information.

An extreme example for these factors can again be found on Oct. 19, 1987. Index futures sold and closed about 10 per cent below the concurrently reported level of the stock index, in spite of the fact that the spot-futures parity shows they should sell higher.[209]

These considerations are especially important for portfolio insurance. Portfolio insurers who synthesized puts had enormous problems in implementing their strategy on Black Monday. The above mentioned points combined with high market impact costs and large bid-ask spreads in effect created very high transaction costs. In addition, the jumps in the price movement violated the continuity assumption of the BS hedging strategy.[210]

The use of traded index options instead of synthetic PI avoids these risks. However, the valuation of these options is made very difficult when the above factors are present, especially in extreme market situations. Hence, it is not always easy to tell whether the market price of a traded index option is too high or too low compared to

---

[209] See Rubinstein (1988): op. cit., p. 39.

[210] See ibid. p. 39.

the cost of synthetic PI (which is again difficult to accurately determine). Empirical evidence on index option prices will be presented in Chapter 8.

Synthetic portfolio insurance is nonetheless still widely used. It offers some features that cannot be obtained by using traded stock or index options. As mentioned before, dynamic hedging can produce a much larger variety of striking prices and maturities than are currently available in traded options. In fact, one can even synthesize nonlinear payoff schemes that are unattainable when simply using fixed positions in options. Also, futures contracts are very liquid, thus often involving smaller market impact costs than found in the options market.[211] Synthetic PI is also a way around the option position limits that were discussed above. But the main reasons for the persistence of synthetic PI appear to be the limited available maturities and the American nature of traded options. The limited maturities of up to nine months make it necessary to roll over a position in traded puts in order to protect a portfolio value for a longer time horizon. In addition, the American nature of traded options makes them more expensive than equivalent European options because of possible early exercise, which

---

[211] See Duffie: Futures Markets, op. cit., p. 296.

however the portfolio insurer is not interested in.[212]

4.12. Recapitulation and Implications

This chapter has given a broad overview of the most important deviations from the ideal and perfect market environment that the option arbitrage relationships and valuation models are based on. The presentation has clarified that the transaction costs incurred when buying or selling stocks, options or futures don't just consist of explicit fees and commissions, but of implicit components as well. The explicit transaction costs are lowest for option market makers and for traders with a seat on the stock exchange. The implicit transaction costs such as the bid-ask spread are usually borne by every market participant, although portfolio insurers and institutional investors with their large orders obviously have the greatest problems with market impact costs and position limits.

Consequently, option market makers and stock market traders are the most advantageously placed candidates for the pursuit of arbitrage profits. An estimate of the

---

212 See Rubinstein, Mark: Alternative paths to portfolio insurance, in: FAJ (July-August 1985b), pp. 42-52, here pp. 46-49. Comment: Rolling over short-term options at first glance seems equivalent to buying a (not available) long-term option, except for the additional transaction costs. However, Rubinstein shows that this strategy lowers the expected return from the insured portfolio. This point will not be elaborated here because it would carry the discussion too far away from the focus of this chapter.

explicit and implicit costs they incur is the benchmark for assessing the real-world profitability of a theoretical arbitrage opportunity.

Transaction costs create a band around the theoretical bounds and arbitrage relationships such as the put-call parity or the box spread. Within that band, violations cannot be arbitraged away. Empirical evidence on the bounds and arbitrage relationships will be presented in Chapter 6.

With respect to option valuation through replication, two crucial problems arise from transaction costs: For one, they will approach infinity in the theoretical case of continuous rebalancing. This can be avoided by rebalancing after reasonably short discrete intervals (e.g. daily). However, discrete rebalancing makes the replication strategy risky, and the argument that the hedging error from discrete adjustments in small intervals is diversifiable does not reconstitute an arbitrage opportunity in the strict sense of the word.

Secondly, there still remains the problem of path-dependency, because the magnitude of the portfolio adjustments depends on the change in the hedge ratio and therefore on the entire path the stock price takes until option maturity.

Nonstationary stock volatility as well as packages of

information that result in jumps are neither transaction costs nor market imperfections. However, any such deviations from geometric Brownian motion, although irrelevant for the bounds and arbitrage relationships, are a significant problem for option valuation with the BS model.

An option pricing model that includes all the different types of transaction costs or trading impediments as separate variables has not yet been developed. Nevertheless, it is important to recognize the effects that short sale restrictions, position limits, market impact costs, deviations from spot-futures parity etc. can have. These factors can be of essential significance when it comes to assessing whether a theoretical arbitrage opportunity is actually profitable in reality. This argument is very important with respect to empirical testing. However, the simultaneous influence of all these factors and the difficulty to determine their respective magnitude mostly prevents researchers from assigning a particular observation to one particular factor. Often, only one specific aspect of the market environment is studied under exclusion of all other influences, or a general measure of "the" transaction costs is invoked. For this reason, many of the effects presented in this chapter could only be discussed in a rather casual manner.

Nonetheless, some of the factors that were addressed have been investigated in greater detail in empirical testing because they can help explain some systematic biases that were found when comparing BS values to actual market prices. Chapter 7 will examine these biases. Changing volatility plays a major role in their explanation. Also, taxes and dividends can explain some of the results and will hence be investigated in greater detail in that context. Amendments and alternatives to the BS model that incorporate jumps and changing volatility in order to capture the biases are discussed in Chapter 8.

5. EMPIRICAL TESTING AND THE EFFICIENT MARKET HYPOTHESIS

5.1. Normal versus Above Normal Returns

A major concept in the context of efficient markets is the difference between normal and above-normal profits. Above-normal profits are returns in excess of the risk-free rate if the strategy is riskless, or in excess of the risk-adjusted rate if the return is uncertain.[213]

With respect to market efficiency, it must be recognized that an equilibrium without apparent arbitrage opportunities is inconsistent with an environment where arbitrage is a costly activity. There will be an "equilibrium degree of inefficiency" that compensates speculators for acquiring costly information, for the cost of buying a seat on the exchange, and for the opportunity costs from devoting their time and work to their activity. However, the risk-adjusted return they get from this activity should be <u>normal</u>.[214]

This is the main point for market efficiency. A market is efficient as long as no trader and no trading rule can consistently produce abnormal, risk-adjusted profits after

---

[213] Risk adjustment, however, is also determined by a model, such as the Capital Asset Pricing Model. Therefore, tests that consider above-normal risky returns are in effect also a joint test of the risk adjustment model.

[214] See Marshall: Futures and Option Contracting, op. cit., p. 270.

taxes and transaction costs.[215]

If above-normal returns cannot be obtained even though a theoretical arbitrage relationship that ignores market imperfections seems to be out of line, one cannot reject that this relationship holds. On the other hand, the precision of the relationship or valuation model is lowered when imperfections allow market prices to deviate from it without giving rise to abnormal return opportunities.

5.2. Synchronous versus Nonsynchronous Prices

Since trading does not take place continuously in real markets, the last price quotes reported for stocks and options can reflect transactions that took place at different times. Continuous, parallel trading of stocks and their options is not a necessary precondition for market efficiency. However, reported prices that are out of line but were registered at different times may make markets look inefficient, whereas the prices actually are merely nonsynchronous.[216]

---

[215] See Galai (1983): Survey, op. cit., p. 46.

[216] See Galai (1983): Survey, op. cit., p. 47.

5.3. Ex Post versus Ex Ante Profits

If a trader were able to implement an arbitrage trade at the same time and prices that constitute the profit opportunity, a so-called ex post test would be suitable. However, this is impossible from the viewpoint of a trader or market maker. He might see at time T that prices are out of line. Based on this signal, he will then build up his arbitrage position at time T+1, but at prices that are unknown at time T and might have moved away so far that the arbitrage opportunity even turns into a loss. Therefore, ex ante tests that recognize this delay are appropriate in determining whether there are profitable deviations in the market.[217]

This aspect points out the arbitrage paradox: Arbitrage is never a riskless activity because trading based on the observed prices at time T will result in a risky position due to the price uncertainty at time T+1. The sure profit opportunity is not sure at all because its implementability is not sure.

---

[217] See Galai, Dan: Empirical tests of boundary conditions for CBOE options, in: JFEC 6 (1978), pp. 187-211, here p. 194.

5.4. Joint Tests and the Validity of Valuation Models

Chapter 4 has pointed out that reality does not conform to the strict assumptions the BS model is based on. Yet, the validity of the BS model or any other alternative should not be completely judged by the assumptions' approximation of the real world. The crucial test is empirical evidence that the model can predict future events better than any competing one.[218]

Even if real world prices deviate from the values predicted by the model, this does not necessarily reject it. For one, the ex ante condition and the problem of market synchronization have to be recognized. Then, there are of course the effects of transaction costs and other market imperfections. It is impossible to reject the validity of the model if the observed prices lie within the bounds that these factors create around the model values.[219]

Nevertheless, it might in fact be the case that tests reveal prices outside these bounds. This could result in above-normal profits that are evidence in <u>support</u> of the model and <u>against</u> the efficiency of the market. In an efficient market, no trading rule, and therefore also none

---

[218] See ibid. p. 48.

[219] See Figlewski (1989a): op. cit., p. 14.

based on an option valuation model or arbitrage relationship, can provide above-normal returns.

Still, even if one model should be found to produce abnormal profits, some other model may work even better. The problem connected with valuation model tests is that they are in effect joint tests of model validity, market efficiency, data accuracy, and risk adjustment concepts.[220] On the other hand, since the bounds and arbitrage relationships are pure dominance arguments that don't involve any valuation concept, their validity should be undisputable if investors prefer more wealth to less. This makes their testing "only" a joint test of data accuracy, risk adjustment, and market efficiency.

220 See Galai (1983): Survey, op. cit., p. 48.

6. EMPIRICAL TESTING OF BOUNDS AND ARBITRAGE RELATIONSHIPS

Empirical tests of the bounds and arbitrage relationships presented in Chapter 2 confront their theoretical precision with the real market environment.

The bounds and arbitrage relationships are pure dominance arguments that don't involve any valuation concept. If violations of them do produce above-normal risk-adjusted profits after transaction and opportunity costs, and inaccurate data due to nonsynchronization or improper transaction cost adjustment can be ruled out, the market must be inefficient. In addition, such a finding also precludes any conformance of market prices with the values predicted by valuation models. This is because the models require an array of additional assumptions that are irrelevant for the bounds and arbitrage relationships, where investors must only prefer more wealth to less.[221]

Since the stock options traded in the United States are dividend unprotected American options, the possibility of early exercise is always a problem when testing the bounds and the European version of the put-call parity. Therefore, early exercise and adjustment to dividends is frequently addressed in the context of the empirical investigations reported below.

---

[221] See Galai (1983): Survey, op. cit., p. 50.

Apart from investigations of the put-call parity, there is more emphasis on calls than on puts. This reflects the fact that the attention in the literature has focused on call options, mainly because put-call parity makes the put price a simple function of the call price (although only precise for European options). Another reason is the greater significance of call trading in light of the fact that put trading volume has historically been relatively small.[222]

6.1. Tests of the Lower Bound for Calls

The minimum value of an American call is bounded by dominance arguments that were presented in Chapter 2.1.4. The pseudo-American lower bound is the tightest possible argument that was established.[223] For more precise estimations of the call value, a valuation model is necessary.

Tests of the European dividend adjusted lower bound and the pseudo-American lower bound have been performed by Galai (1978) and Bhattacharya (1983). They both use data from trades on the CBOE. A violation of the bounds is

---

[222] See ibid. p. 69.

[223] See Galai (1978): op. cit., p. 192.

exploited by buying the call, shorting the stock, and lending.

Galai's data comprises 16,327 daily option and stock closing prices from April through November 1973, the year trading began on the CBOE. Galai ignores transaction costs. The use of closing prices gives rise to the problem of nonsynchronous data. Also, it is assumed that short sales are unrestricted, or alternatively that restrictions to short sales can be circumvented by reducing portfolio long positions. The assumption that the dividends paid on the stocks were known in advance with certainty is a source for potential errors. Finally, Galai checks only the mispricing magnitude, i.e. he doesn't follow the prices in the positions until possible early exercise, worthless expiration or exercise at maturity. Therefore, the testing procedure does not explicitly grasp the respective different transaction costs that are incurred according to the final termination of the position.

Ex post, assuming a flat interest rate of 10 per cent, Galai finds 587 violations of the pseudo-American bound in his sample. 567 of them also don't conform to the weaker European lower bound $c \geq S-Ke^{-rt}-PV(D)$, with an average violation of \$38.10.[224] This average decreased to \$36.30 by using the concurrent treasury bill rate, and the number of violations of the European lower bound decreased to 482, which is 2.95% of the sample.[225]

Only the European bound is tested ex ante. It is assumed that the arbitrage position would be implemented at next day's closing prices. Interestingly, about three quarters of the violations still prevail at implementation an entire day later. However, the ex ante average profit is lowered to about \$12.

Phillips and Smith (1980) argue that the bid-ask spread alone that is incurred when implementing the position would have been sufficient to eliminate the profit. This does not even take transaction costs, uncertainty about future dividends, or any other of the factors discussed in Chapter 4 into account. Also, the reported average ex ante profits are small relative to their dispersion (the profit standard deviation per stock ranges from \$21.40 to \$ 146).[226] This indicates the risk involved when implementing the arbitrage position. Overall, the results are a strong case for market

---

[224] An overall amount for the pseudo-American condition is not given. While the European lower bound is tested on all observations, the pseudo-American bound is only tested on the subset of the overall data where the stocks paid dividends. This subset yields 115 ex post violations averaging \$46, but only 20 of them do not also violate the European bound.

[225] See Galai (1978): op. cit., p. 199.

[226] See ibid. p. 209.

efficiency even right after the opening of the CBOE.

An interesting result to note is that 90 per cent of the violations occurred within 2 months to maturity, and more than 50 per cent within one month. Galai explains this result with the fact that in-the-money options follow stock price movements very closely when maturity is approached, and hence, the result might reflect nonsynchronous data employed in the test.[227] However, this explanation does not seem very convincing. Obviously, one should always expect more violations closer to maturity because the time value (premium above intrinsic value) of the option decreases, thus causing its price to drop closer to its lower bounds.

Bhattacharya (1983) uses CBOE data containing every reported transaction and bid-ask quote from August 1976 until June 1977. In contrast to Galai's use of closing prices, there are on average over 35,000 raw observations per day. Meticulous care is taken to screen the observations in order to avoid errors arising from obvious reporting errors, nonsynchronous data, or quotes with zero volume. After the screening, an impressive data base of 86,137 observations is left for analysis.

The bid-ask spread is explicitly included in the bounds

---

[227] See ibid. pp. 199-200.

by using the relevant bid or ask quotes when establishing the relationships. Refining Galai's approach, Bhattacharya checks more than merely the magnitude of the deviation from these adjusted bounds. In the ex ante tests, the arbitrage position is implemented at the next available prices with nonzero trading volume and liquidated by optimally exercising the call early or holding on until maturity. If the call is exercised, no bid-ask spread costs on the stock acquisition are incurred. If $S^*<K$ at maturity, the call expires worthless and the shorted stock is bought back at the available ask price. This explicit recognition of the final outcome serves to record the incurred bid-ask spreads at termination. Also, the estimated fees that are incurred can thus be imputed more accurately. Bhattacharya estimates fees of $.36 per option contract for market makers and $.80 for stock market arbitrageurs. Per round lot of stock, $4.50 are determined for the market maker and $1 for the arbitrageur.[228]

The explicit recognition of the bid-ask spread as well as the care taken to rule out nonsynchronous data have the result that a lower percentage of the observations generate violations when compared to Galai's (1978) findings. Also, the mispricing magnitude is lower.

---

[228] See Bhattacharya, Mihir: Transactions data tests of efficiency of the Chicago Board Options Exchange, in: JFEC 12 (1983), pp. 161-185, here pp. 167-171.

However, the reduction of the execution lag to the next available trade (compared to 1 day in Galai's test) favors the trader's potential profits. Nonetheless, the ex ante profit for the European lower bound is only $5.17 per contract on average and would have vanished by considering the transaction fees. The pseudo-American bound is tested on the subset of data pertaining to dividend paying stocks. Again, the average profit of $8.20 turns into a loss once the fees are imputed.[229]

Similar to Galai's results, the dispersion of the profit magnitude is substantial, indicating risk. The results show that the positions can generate profits as well as losses of more than $25 per contract.[230] Again, the majority of the mispricing signals come from options close to maturity (42% at less than one week to expiration). Since nonsynchronous data is less likely compared to Galai's procedure, Bhattacharya suspects that these signals occur because investors may sell their in-the-money calls at a discount in order to avoid the far higher round trip transaction costs in the stock they would incur upon exercise.[231]

---

229 See ibid p. 178-179.

230 See ibid. p. 178 and p. 180.

231 See ibid. p. 177.

In both tests, abnormal returns are eliminated by adding back just a few of the costs and restrictions we have discussed. In addition, the reported profits are not even riskless because of the uncertainty concerning the prices the trader gets at implementation. This point is supported by the wide dispersion of the profits found.

In short, the evidence strongly suggests that abnormal returns from violations of the investigated bounds are not obtainable.

6.2. <u>Tests of Put-Call Parity</u>

Gould and Galai (1974) test the put-call parity relationship using data from the late 1960's. They pertain to the dividend protected[232] over the counter options traded by dealers of the Put and Call Brokers and Dealers Association before the creation of the CBOE. The tests are only ex post and in addition are flawed by nonsynchronous observations, but early exercise is taken into account.

Although the over the counter market was not as well-organized as the CBOE or the stock market, most of the observed violations would have been eliminated by fees and

---

[232] Dividend protection means that the striking price is adjusted downward appropriately when the dividend is paid.

bid-ask spreads.[233] Gould and Galai have doubts about the efficiency of the market in the face of the remaining arbitrage opportunities, which are sometimes of surprising magnitude. However, the nonsynchronous data and the failure to carry out the test on an ex ante basis should make it impossible to prove market inefficiency with these results.

Klemkosky and Resnik (1980) conduct an ex ante test of put-call parity using trade by trade CBOE data from selected days between July 1977 and June 1978. Since CBOE options are not dividend protected, early exercise causes tricky problems in the test. In perfect market conditions, a long hedge established by writing a call, buying a put, buying the stock and borrowing Ke^{-rt}+PV(D) should not be profitable if early exercise is excluded. This strategy is equivalent to converting a put and selling the call. The exclusion of early exercise at all times to maturity for both the put and the call would reestablish the European put-call parity because the early exercise feature of the American options must be worthless. The terminal profit should be zero or negative, i.e:[234]

[233] See Gould, J.P. / Galai, Dan: Transaction costs and the relationship between put and call prices, in: JFEC 1 (1974), pp. 105-129, here p. 123.

[234] See Klemkosky, Robert C. / Resnik, Bruce G.: An ex ante analysis of put-call parity, in: JFEC 8 (1980), pp. 363-378, here p. 365.

$(C-P-S)e^{rt}+K+PV(D)e^{rt} \leq 0$

Since the authors neglect to point out the potential effects of possible early exercise on the observed option prices, we should add these considerations at this point: If early exercise of the call is precluded at all times, this makes early exercise of the put possible (see Section 2.2.). Thus, the put value is raised above its European value, resulting in a higher required investment for the put and an even more negative payoff from the hedge.[235] This statement relies on the assumption that the hedger never exercises the put early (not even if it is optimal) and hence holds the portfolio until maturity. Klemkosky and Resnik adhere to this assumption in their tests.[236] This biases the results downward but also recognizes that early exercise during the life of an option cannot be predetermined with certainty in advance, because actual early exercise depends first and foremost on the question whether the option is in the money. Therefore, profits arising from optimal early exercise of the put option held would not be certain and hence not riskless.

Klemkosky and Resnik also recognize the cases where the written call is exercised early against the hedger, an

---

[235] See Gladstein/Merton/Scholes (1982): op. cit., p. 17.

[236] See Klemkosky/Resnik (1980): op. cit., p. 366.

action on which the hedger does not have any influence. This results in an earlier reception of the striking price for the hedger, but also causes the loss of dividends because the stock must be delivered. The lost dividends are higher than the gained interest on the striking price when early exercise of calls is optimal. Hence, the hedge return is lowered, conservatively assuming that the hedger's put will be valueless at early exercise of the call.[237] But the resulting dispersion in the returns from the conversion, depending on whether the call is exercised early or not, obviously makes the conversions a risky investment.[238] In their testing approach, the authors however neglect that the initially received price for the written American call should be higher than implied by the European put-call parity if early exercise of the call is possible. The thus raised terminal conversion return may well be positive without indicating a violation. The use of data where the put, the call or both may be exercised early obviously distorts the results when the (in this case no longer applicable) European put-call parity is used.

Of the 606 examined hedges, 147 yield ex post returns in excess of the $20 estimated round trip fees for

---

237 See Klemkosky/Resnik (1980): op. cit., p. 369.

238 See Gladstein/Merton/Scholes (1982): op. cit., p. 17.

exchange members. Ex ante, with execution lags of 5 and 15 minutes, most of these observations would still have been profitable, but to a lesser degree than ex post.[239]

Only a few of the ex ante profits are larger than the $70 transaction costs that are estimated when the bid-ask spread is included. And these remaining profits are still risky as shown above, and affected by the problems of legging in, uncertain dividend expectations, and possible interference from the other factors discussed in Chapter 4. Fortunately, the addressed distortions connected with early exercise of the written call don't seem to have significantly affected the results, because early exercise of the call is shown to occur only in 8 sample conversions.[240] Concerning the rapidity of price adjustments in the market, the 15 minute lags reduce profits more than the 5 minute lags.[241] This supports the notion of rapid price correction and market efficiency.

A short hedge or reversal is also checked for violations. A put is written and hedged with the replicating position of long the call, short the stock and lending Ke^{-rt}+PV(D). Assuming no early exercise of the

---

[239]See ibid. p. 370.

[240]See ibid. p. 369.

[241]See ibid. p. 372.

options, the terminal payoff should again be negative:[242]

$$(P-C+S)e^{rt}-K-PV(D)e^{rt} \le 0$$

Again, the price effects of early exercise should be examined more closely than done by the authors. If early exercise of the put can be precluded at all times to maturity, early exercise of the call is possible (see Section 2.2.), i.e. one cannot simultaneously preclude early exercise for both the American call and put. This raises the value of the call that is bought above its European value, resulting in an even more negative hedge payoff. However, total preclusion of early put exercise is unrealistic because it would require a dividend payment right at expiration to keep $PV(D)>K-Ke^{-rt}$ at all times. In the absence of such a payment, the written put may be exercised early. When early put exercise is not ruled out, and if the early exercise possibility of the call right before an ex-dividend date is not checked separately (which the authors don't do), the sample may encompass reversals where the call, the put or both may be rationally exercised early. Possible early exercise of American options raises their value above that of their European version. If consequently the written put value is raised, but not the call value, the reversal return will rise. If both option values are raised because early

---

[242] See ibid. p. 373.

exercise can't be precluded for either one of them, the deviations from European put-call parity and hence the resulting effect on the return from the reversal is equivocal. If the put value is raised more than the call value, the return will rise, and vice versa.

This rather elaborate discussion is necessary to reiterate that the price effects on American options arising from possible early exercise can severely distort the results when the European put-call parity is tested on them, as done and mostly ignored by Klemkosky and Resnik.

In the authors' reversal test, the hedger is assumed to hold the call until maturity, even if its early exercise might be optimal, which biases the results downward. Also, the cases where the written put is actually exercised early against the hedger are considered. This results in an earlier date to pay the striking price, but also requires diminished restitution for the dividends on the shorted stock. When early exercise of the put is rational, the dividend payments saved by the hedger must be less than the foregone interest on the striking price. Hence, as before, the hedge return will be lowered, conservatively assuming that the hedger's call will be valueless at early exercise of the put.[243] This line of reasoning again ignores the initially higher American put

---

[243] See ibid. p. 375.

price received when it was written, i.e. the terminal hedge payoff can now be positive without constituting a true violation. Also, similar to the conversions, the resulting dispersion in the profits, depending on whether the written put is actually exercised early, makes the reversals risky.

Of the 148 short hedges, only a few have ex ante returns above the $70 of estimated fees and bid-ask spreads. Again, the profits for the 15 minute lags are lower than for 5 minutes, indicating quick price adjustment. However, in contrast to the conversion test, the price effects of early exercise of the written put may have considerably distorted the results: 52 of the 148 sample reversals are shown to be prematurely terminated.[244]

For the same reasons as the arbitrage with long hedges, the reversal returns are risky, and factors other than the bid-ask spread and fees are ignored. In particular, the ignored early exercise effects on the prices and the denial of proceeds from the stock short sale could make actual, risk-adjusted short hedge returns lower than those estimated in the test. The remaining profits thus cannot be regarded as above-normal.[245]

---

[244] See ibid. p. 376.

[245] See ibid. p. 377.

Overall, the results of put-call parity testing reject the existence of abnormal return opportunities and strongly suggest market efficiency with respect to this arbitrage relationship.

6.3. Tests of the Call Convexity Condition

Galai (1979) tests the call convexity condition on closing prices of CBOE options that traded in 1973, the opening year of the exchange. Among about 1000 observed option triplets, only 24 violations of the convexity condition are found. Checking these by examining the corresponding prices during the trading day reveals that most of the violations appeared for the closing prices only. This indicates that most of the deviations may have been caused by nonsynchronous data.[246]

The results are a very strong case for market efficiency because even in a newly opened market, ex post, and ignoring transaction costs or other imperfections, violations of the convexity condition were hardly found.

Bhattacharya (1983) conducts a test on the call convexity condition using trade by trade CBOE data from 1977. To rule out nonsynchronization problems, only option price

[246] See Galai (1979): op. cit., p. 87.

triplets observed during time spans where the underlying stock price remained unchanged are regarded as eligible for providing violation signals.

Among 1006 triplets, only one minor violation is found, thus again strongly supporting market efficiency even without considering transaction costs or ex ante implementation.[247]

6.4. Tests of the Box Spread Arbitrage Relationship

Ronn and Ronn (1989) test the box spread condition on intraday CBOE data pertaining to eight trading days between 1977 and 1984. The bid-ask spread is explicitly recognized in the condition when checking for violation signals. Data nonsynchronization does not seem to play a major role. The reason is that the underlying stock price is shown not to change much during the one-hour time intervals that are investigated for constructing a box spread position with the appropriate two calls and puts.

Ex post, and ignoring fees, the implied lending rates are frequently higher than the concurrent treasury bill rates.[248] Ex ante, these opportunities remain mostly unchanged if the recognition lag required for analyzing

---

[247]See Bhattacharya (1983): op. cit., p. 179.

[248]See Ronn/Ronn (1989): op. cit., p. 98.

the signals and issuing the arbitrage orders is set at 5 minutes. However, a lag of ten minutes usually results in the entire elimination of above-T-bill returns.[249]

The quick adjustment of the prices supports the notion of CBOE efficiency. Another noteworthy result is the minor economic magnitude of the violations. Even assuming immediate implementability at the violation prices (which amounts to an ex post consideration), and using the entire observed number of transactions as the implemented trading volume, the total realized excess interest on investment would have been between $16 and $12,369 on the eight selected days. In the face of the ignored fees, the opportunity costs for detecting the violations and executing the trades, and risks in legging in and out, these ex post profits seem economically insignificant.[250]

The same results are found for the OEX 100 stock index option, even taking into account that the incurred transaction costs at expiration are zero because of the cash settlement.

---

[249] See ibid. p. 102.

[250] See ibid. p. 103.

6.5. Implications

The tests reported above represent the most rigorous examinations to date of dominance bounds and arbitrage relationships for stock options. Their results have been presented under conscious consideration of transaction costs and risk that influence the profitability of their violations. The evidence cannot reject that the relationships hold. None of the tests can prove the existence of above-normal profits. Hence, the way is paved for empirical testing of option valuation models with their far stronger underlying assumptions.

However, an insight gained from the results reported above is that violations of theoretical relationships are not ruled out per se. Except for the strong performance of the convexity condition, the theoretical precision of the relationships is obviously blurred by transaction costs and numerous other factors that create a band around them.

7. EMPIRICAL EVIDENCE ON THE BLACK-SCHOLES MODEL: THE PRICING BIASES

When comparing BS values to market prices, one frequently finds systematic deviations. They are related to the degree the respective option is in or out-of-the-money, and sometimes to the time to expiration.

This chapter presents empirical evidence on these pricing biases and explores whether they are a sign for exploitable market inefficiencies. All major work to date has been conducted on CBOE calls, and therefore only evidence pertaining to this set of data is reported.

Following the evidence, factors that might explain the deviations if the market in fact prices options efficiently will be discussed. The biases have prompted the development of more complex valuation models. They are addressed in Chapter 8.

7.1. Empirical Results on Striking Price Biases

While the uncertainty about future interest rates can be alleviated for all practical purposes by using the T-bill rate for the same maturity as the option (see Section 4.3.), the future volatility is the single input variable that is not readily observable. When solving the BS model for the standard deviation implied in option market prices (ISD), this ISD actually serves as a free parameter. It impounds not only the market's expectation of future stock volatility, but also any influences that systematically affect this volatility, as well as any other factors that are not recognized in the model as separate variables.[251] If such factors exist in reality, they will cause biases.

Evidence that the assumption of constant (or deterministic) volatility is unrealistic has been presented before and will be complemented below and in the next chapter. Hence, it is not surprising that ISD's are found to differ across option maturities. They thereby impound different market expectations of the stock's volatility over the respective life of the option.[252] However, options with the same maturity, differing only in the striking price, should display the <u>same</u> implied volatility.[253]

Yet, empirical evidence shows significant differences in ISD's across striking prices. The testing approach is to assume that the option market is efficient. In addition, it is assumed that the BS model correctly prices at-the-money options, using its ISD as a benchmark to

---

[251] See Figlewski (1989a): op. cit., p. 13.

[252] See Chance, Don M.: Empirical tests of the pricing of index call options, in: Advances in Futures and Options Research, Volume 1, Part A (1986), pp. 141-166, here p. 151.

[253] See Bhattacharya (1983): op. cit., p. 165.

discern over- and underpricing.[254] The use of the at-the-money ISD as benchmark is based on comments in Black (1975) and supported by some empirical evidence on its predictive performance, which will be elaborated on in Chapter 8. A higher implied volatility for in- or out-of-the-money options means that the model underprices them. Conversely, a lower implied volatility indicates overpricing.

Black (1975) observes that the model systematically underpriced out-of-the-money CBOE calls in the period from 1973 to 1975, while overpricing in-the-money calls.

Subsequently, Macbeth and Merville (1979) conduct an elaborate test on call options traded on six stocks in the entire year 1976. In order to exclude early exercise effects, they eliminate any options that would have been exercised early according to the pseudo-American formula from their sample.

In contrast to Black, they find that implied variance rates decline as the exercise price increases, i.e. the model overprices out-of-the-money options and underprices

---

[254] Note that this approach uses Black-Scholes values as pricing equations.

in-the-money options.[255] (Also, their evidence confirms the nonstationarity of volatility, because the ISD's are found to change from day to day.)

Depending on the option and the time to expiration, the in-the-money ISD was often four times higher than the deep-out-of-the-money ISD. This results in considerable percentage deviations of the market prices from model values computed with the at-the-money benchmark volatility. For example, the mean deviation in per cent of the Black-Scholes value for IBM options with more than 90 days to expiration was as follows: on average, out-of-the-money prices were 7% lower than the BS values, while in-the-money prices were 6% higher.[256] Generally, the percentage deviations appear greater for out-of-the-money options (the average for each stock often exceeds 10%). However, since their prices are small compared to in-the-money options, the $ deviation is larger for in-the-money options.

Rubinstein (1985a) examines all CBOE calls on 30 stocks traded in the period between August 1976 and August 1978. Again, options with likely early exercise according to the

---

[255] See Macbeth, James D. / Merville, Larry J.: An empirical examination of the Black-Scholes call option pricing model, in: JOF 34 (1979), pp. 1173-1186, here p. 1185.

[256] See ibid. p. 1183.

pseudo-American formula are discarded from the sample.

The results of his test are striking:
Until Oct. 21, 1977, the bias discovered by Macbeth and Merville (1979) continued, with the implied volatility declining the higher the striking price. However, beginning on Oct. 24, 1977, and persisting until the end of the sample period, the bias is exactly reversed, with the ISD increasing the higher the striking price. Thus, in this second period, Black's (1975) original bias is restored.

In both periods, the respective bias is significant at the 99.9 per cent level of confidence.[257] Most of the resulting price deviations in the sample are below 5%.

Chance (1986) examines the pricing bias in the OEX 100 index call option traded on the CBOE on data from the first four months of 1984. Since the underlying index contains 100 stocks that don't all pay dividends at the same time, the continuous dividend yield is regarded appropriate as a dividend adjustment (see Chapter 3). Problems with early exercise are reported to be unlikely (although not completely eliminated).

Chance finds the striking price bias to be back to

---

[257] See Rubinstein, Mark: Nonparametric tests of alternative option pricing models using all reported trades and quotes on the 30 most active CBOE option classes from August 23, 1976 through August 31, 1978, in: JOF 40 (1985a), pp. 455-480, here p. 474.

Macbeth and Merville's (1979) relationship: the ISD's decline with higher exercise prices, thus causing the BS model to underprice in-the-money calls and overprice out-of-the-money calls. On average, in-the-money ISD's are 15.67% higher than the at-the-money benchmark, while out-of-the-money ISD's are 18.02% lower. The resulting average deviation of BS values (computed with the at-the-money ISD) from market prices in the sample is -3% for in-the-money options and +14.4% for out-of-the-moneys.[258]

7.2. Comments on the Time to Expiration Bias

All the above tests also reveal some relationships between the ISD and the time to maturity. Again, the findings are often contradictory, but the results are not as systematic as those revealed for the striking price bias. Some tests reveal reversals of biases depending on whether the investigated options with different maturities are in- or out-of-the-money. Others find discernible time to expiration biases to be confined to <u>only</u> in- or out-of-the-money options. The only fairly consistent result of the above discussed tests is that the ISD of in-the-money options is higher the closer to expiration they are (i.e.

[258] See Chance (1986): op. cit., p. 153.

the BS model underprices them).[259] This will be referred to as "the" time to expiration bias in the remainder of this thesis.

Rubinstein (1985a), however, cannot confirm any conclusive maturity bias for in-the-money options. But across both of his examination periods, he finds short maturity out-of-the-money calls to be underpriced by the BS model.[260] This result is somewhat surprising, because Macbeth/Merville (1979), whose sample period partly coincides with Rubinstein's, find them to be overpriced.[261] Also, the BS model tends to overprice at-the-money short maturity calls in Rubinstein's first period, while they are underpriced in the second period.[262]

Chiras and Manaster (1978), whose spread test will be presented in greater detail in Section 7.4., find short maturity options in general to be on average underpriced by the BS model.[263] Their data pertains to the period from June 1973 through April 1975. Their results

---

[259] See Black (1975): op. cit., p. 64; Macbeth/Merville (1979): op. cit., p. 1175; Chance (1986): op. cit., p. 151.

[260] See Rubinstein (1985a): op. cit., p. 474.

[261] See Macbeth/Merville (1979): op. cit., p. 1175.

[262] See Rubinstein (1985a): op. cit., p. 474.

[263] See Chiras, Donald P. / Manaster, Steven: The information content of option prices and a test of market efficiency, in: JFEC 6 (1978), pp. 213-234, here p. 231.

corroborate the identical observations in Black (1975).[264]

As mentioned before, different ISD's across maturities are not surprising when stock volatility is nonstationary. Some of the tests give an indication of this nonstationarity because they find that the ISD's change through time.[265] The market will accordingly have different estimates of the future stock volatility pertaining to different time horizons. Therefore, relationships to the time to maturity needn't necessarily be a bias.[266]

If other factors that influence the ISD across maturities do exist, they will be difficult to discern if the stock volatility estimate itself changes. This may explain why the findings concerning time to expiration biases are less clear-cut and consistent. Yet, it is hard to explain the remaining discernible, fairly persistent bias reported above with different volatility expectations alone. Why should the volatility expectation at any time during the sample periods in several tests be higher the shorter the time to maturity: is it realistic that the

---

[264] Neither Chiras/Manaster (1978) nor Black (1975) specify whether this bias is confined to short maturity options that are in- or out-of-the-money to a particular degree.

[265] See for example Macbeth/Merville (1979): op. cit., p. 1174 as well as Chance (1986): op. cit., pp. 152-153.

[266] One possible explanation for this phenomenom may be the casual observation that stock volatility rises near option expiration because the closing of positions and the exercise of options affects the underlying stock prices. In the markets, this is often mentioned in the context of the "triple witching hour", when futures contracts, stock options and index options simultaneously expire.

stock volatility should always drop more and more the further into the future we go? Why is this bias consistent across several tests for in-the-money options only, with less obvious or even reversed[267] time to expiration bias for out-of-the-money options?

Section 7.4. will present a possible explanation for this time to expiration bias that is related to the dividend adjustment.

7.3. A Summarizing Overview

To summarize the empirical evidence presented above, this section provides two tables that give an overview of the findings reported by the respective authors. To make the evidence easily comparable, all findings in the tables are given as deviations of BS values from market prices, not as differences in ISD's.

Some of the results in the studies are originally reported in terms of ISD differences only. This avoids having to somewhat arbitrarily determine a benchmark ISD. Rubinstein (1985a) uses this reporting method for all his results. Macbeth/Merville (1979) and Chance (1986) use it

267 See Macbeth/Merville (1979): op. cit., p. 1175. The authors find the time to expiration bias to reverse for out-of-the-money calls.

to report their findings pertaining to time to expiration biases. In the face of a lacking benchmark ISD, "converting" their reporting method for the table hence relies on the following, rather strong assumption: in the respective tests, the BS model is assumed to correctly price at-the-money calls (benchmark for the striking price bias) and longer maturity calls (benchmark for the time to expiration bias). The tables also indicate where sample periods overlap.

a) Striking price biases

Author	BS model <u>underprices</u> out-of-the-money calls and <u>overprices</u> in-the-money calls in the given period	BS model <u>overprices</u> out-of-the-money calls and <u>underprices</u> in-the-money calls in the given period
Black (1975)	about[268] 1973 through July 1975	
Macbeth/ Merville(1979)		Dec.31, 1975 through Dec.31, 1976
		⇑OVERLAP⇓
Rubinstein(85) first period:		Aug.23, 1976 through Oct.21, 1977
Rubinstein(85) second period:	Oct.24, 1977 through Aug.31, 1978	
Chance (1986)		January 1984 through April 1984

268 Black does not specify how he got his results and to which time period they pertain. Yet, the author's observations appear to be related to the CBOE, where trading began in 1973. The article was published in July 1975.

b) Time to expiration biases for short maturity calls that are in-, at-, or out-of-the-money

Author	Period	in-the-money	at-the-money	out-of-the-money
Black (1975)	about 73-July 75	-- underpricing --[a]		
⇑OVERLAP⇓				
Chiras/ Manaster(1978)	June 73 -April 75	-- underpricing --[a]		
Macbeth/ Merville(1979)	Dec.31, 75 -Dec,31, 76	underpricing	not systematic	overpricing
⇑OVERLAP⇓				
Rubinstein(85) first period:	Aug.23, 76 -Oct.21, 77	not systematic	overpricing	underpricing
Rubinstein(85) second period:	Oct.24, 77 -Aug.31, 78	not systematic	underpricing	underpricing
Chance (1986)	Jan. 84 -April 84	underpricing	not systematic	not systematic

[a]No distinction is made by the authors between the degree in- or out-of-the-money.

7.4. Is the Market Wrong? Evidence on Profiting from the Biases

The question that immediately arises when looking at the biases is whether they may point out market inefficiencies that give rise to abnormal return opportunities. If abnormal returns are achievable, taking all the factors presented in Chapter 4 and the problems connected with empirical testing (Chapter 5) into account, market efficiency can be rejected.

However, even in such a case the model validity cannot be unequivocally confirmed, because testing model predictions against market prices is a joint test of model validity and market efficiency. Some other model might yield even higher abnormal returns. Conversely, if the biases don't yield abnormal profits due to the transaction costs and market imperfections, the validity of the BS model cannot be rejected, which however does not mean that it is proved.

7.4.1. Trading Strategies to Exploit the Biases

a) Neutral hedges:

Neutral hedges are the straightforward way to profit from perceived mispricings. If the option price is higher (lower) than the model value, one writes (buys) the option and buys (shorts) $\Delta = N(d_1)$ shares of the underlying stock. If continuous adjustment of the hedge is not feasible, one can invoke the argument of zero systematic risk when looking at a portfolio of discretely adjusted hedges (as long as the adjustment is reasonably frequent).

If prices conformed to BS values in the ideal BS world, such a hedge would earn (or cost) the riskless rate. In the real market environment, any hedge return above the risk-free rate (excess return) is abnormal if it is higher than needed to cover the transaction costs and risks arising from market imperfections.

By writing the option, an investment hedge profits from options that are overpriced in the market compared to the BS model. The resulting excess dollar return per rebalancing interval is:[269]

$$[N(d_1)_0(S_1-S_0) - (C_1-C_0)] - [(N(d_1)_0S_0-C_0)(e^{r\Delta t}-1)]$$

where the subscripts 0 and 1 denote the beginning and end of a rebalancing interval, and Δt is its length.

The excess dollar return from a borrowing hedge that profits from calls underpriced in the market by buying them is:

$$[(C_1-C_0)-N(d_1)_0(S_1-S_0)] - [(C_0-N(d_1)_0S_0)(e^{r\Delta t}-1)]$$

The hedge is maintained and adjusted <u>until expiration</u> of the option, and the excess return per rebalancing interval is computed.[270] Alternatively, one can close the position after each revision interval and immediately reestablish it according to the then prevailing relationship between the market and the model price. (Some tests, e.g. Galai (1977) and Chance (1986), have been performed this way).

---

[269] See Galai, Dan: Tests of market efficiency of the Chicago Board Options Exchange, in: JOB 50 (1977), pp. 167-197, here p. 174.

[270] It should be reiterated at this point that the equations above denote the dollar excess return per revision interval only. This confinement to the revision interval is necessary because the required investment or borrowing amount and hence the interest paid or earned on it changes when the hedge ratio changes. If one wants to determine the entire excess dollar return over the life of the option, the interval profits have to be added up, including the interest earned on them until option maturity.

While such a procedure of course implies higher transaction costs, it also raises the profit because it captures returns from favorable price movements that were uncertain at inception of the hedge.[271] (This aspect will be examined in greater detail in Chapter 9).

b) Spreading:
Instead of using a position in stocks to form the hedge, one can alternatively use another option on the stock, for example with a different striking price (vertical spread) or a different time to expiration (horizontal spread). With stocks, a position in one option is hedged with an offsetting position in $N(d_1)$ shares. Alternatively, $1/N(d_1)$ options hedge one share.

A position of $1/N(d_1)_i$ options of type i hence moves like one share and can be hedged with the opposite position in $1/N(d_1)_j$ options of type j on the same stock, but with different striking price or maturity. With options of type i long and type j short, the spread investment is $1/N(d_1)_i C_i - 1/N(d_1)_j C_j$. For one option C_i long, the investment I is consequently (by multiplying by

[271] If a hedge is established according to an initial mispricing and then rebalanced and held until expiration, the initial mispricing is in effect spread as a profit over the entire time until maturity. Favorable movements in the mispricing (mispricing reductions) until the next rebalancing are canceled by unfavorable ones, because the position is maintained as at inception and should ultimately yield a profit in the magnitude of the initial mispricing when the option expires. However, if the position can be reversed before maturity, additional profits can be reaped from reversals in the mispricing, thus raising the average excess dollar return per rebalancing interval. It must be kept in mind, however, that these returns from the mispricing movements are unknown in advance and hence uncertain.

$N(d_1)_i$):[272]

$$I = C_i - \frac{N(d_1)_i}{N(d_1)_j} C_j$$

Again, the positions are rebalanced appropriately, and no returns (absolute value if negative investment) on I above the riskless rate would be expected under BS assumptions.

Relative over- or underpricing between 2 options can be detected by comparing the ratio of their model prices (superscript BS), to the ratio of their actual market prices (superscript A). One buys option i and sells option j when[273]

$$\frac{C_i^{BS}}{C_j^{BS}} > \frac{C_i^{A}}{C_j^{A}}$$

and vice versa. An even more promising position can be established by shorting an option that is more expensive compared to its BS value and hedging it by going long in another option on that stock that is selling below its BS value.[274]

---

272 See Galai (1977): op. cit., p. 190.

273 See ibid. p. 191.

274 See Chiras, Donald P. / Manaster, Stephen: The Information content of option prices and a test of market efficiency, in: JFEC 6 (1978), pp. 213-234, here p. 230.

c) Prerequisite: getting the Black-Scholes input variables:

S, K and t are all observable, and as mentioned before, the use of T-bills maturing at the same time as the option gives a reasonable estimate for the interest rate. The major unknown is the future volatility of the stock. It is sometimes inferred from historical stock volatility. Others use a weighted average of the ISD's of the options on a stock, or they simply employ the ISD of at-the-money options. Chapter 8 will take a close look at questions pertaining to volatility.

7.4.2. Empirical Evidence on the Trading Strategies

The first test of the BS model was performed by Black and Scholes (1972) on data from over the counter (OTC) options traded between 1966 and 1969. The problem with this data set is that OTC options were only traded when initially written, i.e. there was no secondary market. Hence, Black and Scholes calculate subsequent market prices by using the model values.

The strategy employed is to form neutral hedges with the underlying stock when buying or selling calls that are trading above or below their model values, respectively.[275] The initial position is adjusted daily and maintained until expiration. In effect, maintaining the initial position deprives the arbitrageur from capturing favorable movements in the mispricing before maturity. The test results, reported in average daily excess returns, thus in essence arise from spreading out the initial size of the violation over the entire life of the option.

Historical volatility is used as an estimate for σ. The strategy yields average excess returns of $.56 per contract per day. Even ignoring that these profits are only ex post, the introduction of transaction costs into the analysis eliminates them. Black and Scholes hence conclude that the OTC market was efficient during the sample period.[276]

In order to test the theoretical result that returns on discretely adjusted hedges are uncorrelated with the market, the profits on the daily rebalanced hedges are regressed on the return on the S&P 500 stock index. The β-estimate is insignificantly different from zero, thus

---

[275] The use of model values after inception of the hedge has the effect that all subsequent stock price movements will of course be closely matched by the movements in the option values, thus yielding close to zero excess dollar returns from those days.

[276] See Black, Fischer / Scholes, Myron: The valuation of options and a test of market efficiency, Papers and Proceedings of the Thirtieth Annual Meeting of the American Finance Association, 17-29 Dec. 1971, in: JOF 27 (1972), pp. 399-417, here p. 417.

corroborating the theoretical result as expected.[277]

The first tests of the BS model using CBOE data were performed by Galai (1977). His data consists of daily closing prices for every option traded on the CBOE from April through November 1973, right after the opening of the exchange. Galai performs two hedge tests. In the first test, he repeats the strategy of Black and Scholes (1972) above. The initial position in the hedge is adjusted daily and maintained until maturity, thus again in effect spreading out an initial mispricing. Since the CBOE provides a secondary market, observed option prices can now also be used after hedge inception, in contrast to Black and Scholes' imputed model values. Galai reports an ex post daily return of $1.7 per contract.[278]

Galai's second hedge test takes advantage of the fact that the secondary market for options allows to revise the neutral hedging strategy daily: if initially, the call was underpriced (overpriced) relative to the BS model, it is bought (sold) and an appropriate position in the stock is shorted (held long).[279] On the following day, the position is terminated and immediately reestablished, but

---

[277] See ibid. p. 404.

[278] See Galai (1977): op. cit., p. 176.

[279] The volatilities employed to compute the BS values are based on historical data and on estimates supplied by Myron Scholes.

not necessarily in the original way. If the initially underpriced call is now overpriced by the market, the hedge is reversed, writing the call and buying Δ shares. This strategy makes it possible not only to profit from an initial mispricing, but also from switches in the mispricing during the life of the option.

Ex post, the strategy yields average excess returns per option contract (on 100 shares) of $10 per day.[280] This is an interesting outcome when comparing it to the $1.7 profit in the first test, where the initial position was maintained. The $8.3 rise in profits clearly underscores that the ability to capture favorable mispricing movements is an important feature of an arbitrage position. This aspect will be discussed in Section 9.2.

Like Black and Scholes (1972), Galai finds no correlation with the market when regressing the hedge returns on the S&P 500 index. In a sensitivity analysis, the ex post profits are found to be higher for stocks with low dividend yields, thus showing that the dividend-unadjusted BS formula performs better when its basic assumptions are maintained.[281] The second hedge test is repeated on an ex ante basis, lagging the execution of trades by one day. This cuts the average profit in half,

---

[280] Galai (1977): op. cit., pp. 178-179.

[281] See ibid. p. 182.

to $5 per day.

Galai's analysis ignores transaction costs, is plagued by the closing price nonsimultaneity problem, and does not take any of the other possible obstacles presented in Chapter 4 into account. Also, the returns incorporate profits from favorable movements of the mispricing, which are not sure at inception of the hedge.

Yet, Phillips and Smith (1980) show that the bid-ask spread alone would have been sufficient to eliminate the ex post and ex ante profits, thus rejecting market inefficiency.

Galai (1977) also considers a horizontal spreading strategy, buying or selling call i and hedging it with $N(d_1)_i/N(d_1)_j$ calls j with different maturity. Comparing the model price ratio between the two options to their market price ratio reveals which option to buy and which to sell. The spreads are revised and reestablished daily, again making it possible to reverse the position if the mispricing switches. Ex ante, with one day lags, the average profit is $4 per spread and day.[282] Again, the bid-ask spread alone would have been sufficient to eliminate it.[283]

To check the notion that the BS model undervalues short

---

[282] See ibid. p. 194.

[283] See Phillips/Smith (1980): op. cit., p. 188.

maturity options (the time to expiration bias discussed in Section 7.2.), Galai also performs a spread test where all short maturity options are sold and hedged with longer maturity options. The ex post return is merely $3.1 per spread and day and displays a considerable variability, making it impossible to statistically reject the hypothesis of zero average profits. Thus, the result does not support the time to expiration bias.[284]

Latané and Rendleman (1976) use weekly option and stock closing prices from October 1973 through June 1974. They argue that the ISD's of options further in or out of the money should not be a good representative of the market's assessment of the future stock volatility because their Λ_c is so low, i.e. they are not so sensitive to an incorrect volatility specification. Hence, a weighted average ISD is used as the benchmark where the weights are the respective Λ_c. This benchmark is employed to compute the BS values.

The most underpriced and the most overpriced calls are written and hedged appropriately with the underlying stocks. The positions are closed one week later. As expected, the hedges where calls are written whose market price was above the BS value yields returns in excess of the risk free rate, while the other group performs worse

---

[284]See Galai (1977): op. cit., p. 191.

than a risk free investment. The weekly excess returns, which again capture favorable price movements, average around 3.6% for the hedges with calls overpriced in the market, while the average for those underpriced in the market is -2.8%.[285] However, their standard deviations of 9.8% and 7%, respectively, show that not adjusting the hedges for an entire week induces considerable (but arguably diversifiable) risk.

The authors concede that the data are not free of the nonsimultaneity problem. In addition, the test is only ex post, and transaction costs or bid-ask spreads are ignored. Hence, the test does not appear rigorous enough to reject market efficiency.

Trippi (1977) uses a trading rule that is based on deviations from (arithmetic) average ISD's. The ISD's of all calls on a stock traded on a particular day are computed. The average ISD is then used to compute the BS value for each option. If the market price exceeds (is less than) the BS value by more than 15%, the call is written (bought). The positions are closed one week later.

Trippi uses weekly closing prices from August 1974 through March 1975. All in all, 201 short positions and

---

[285] See Latané, Henry A. / Rendleman, Richard J.: Standard deviations of stock price ratios implied in option prices, in: JOF 31 (1976), pp. 369-381, here p. 375.

202 long positions are triggered. The weekly ex post average return is 11.4%.[286]

While this looks like a handsome profit, Trippi ignores all market imperfections, in particular fees and the bid-ask spread, price nonsynchroneity, and ex ante implementability. Most importantly, his positions are not hedged at all, thus embodying considerable risk.

Phillips and Smith (1980) show that the bid-ask spread alone would reduce the weekly profits by about 6.75%. Taking all the other factors and the riskiness of the strategy into account, one cannot indisputably conclude that the remaining profits are abnormal.

Chiras and Manaster (1978) use the BS model adjusted for constant dividend yield. The data consist of monthly closing prices from June 1973 through April 1975. Like Trippi (1977), Chiras/Manaster compute the ISD's. Instead of using the arithmetic average, a weighing scheme is employed where the option's price elasticity with respect to its ISD is the respective weight. This gives the most weight to the ISD of at-the-money options. The weighted average ISD is used to compute the BS values.

The trading rule is to form horizontal or vertical

---

[286] See Trippi, Robert R.: A test of option market efficiency using a random walk valuation model, in: Journal of Economics and Business 29 (1977), pp. 93-98, here p. 97.

spreads if there simultaneously exist options whose market price exceeds (is less than) the BS value by more than 10%, thus filtering out the positions with the highest profit potential. If option i is overpriced by more than 10%, it is written and hedged with $N(d_1)_i/N(d_1)_j$ options j that are underpriced by more than 10%. The positions are closed one month later, without interim adjustment of the hedge ratios. Although the (substantial) risk caused by not rebalancing might still be diversifiable to some degree, the one month period is obviously a grave departure from continuous trading.

The average ex post monthly spread return is 9.7%.[287] Yet, the bid-ask spread alone would have been sufficient to eliminate it.[288] This clearly rejects the authors' claim that the CBOE was inefficient during the sample period.

An interesting finding, already alluded to in Section 7.2., is that over 78% of the established spreads are horizontal (different times to maturity). Of these horizontal spreads, again 78% are established by writing the shorter maturity option.[289] This indicates that the BS model underpriced short maturity options during the

---

287 See ibid. p. 230.

288 See Phillips/Smith (1980): op. cit., p. 192.

289 See Chiras/Manaster (1978): op. cit., p. 231.

sample period, thus providing evidence for the time to expiration bias. (The authors do not elaborate whether this maturity bias is confined to in- or out-of-the-money options.) However, as just stated, this does not generate abnormal return opportunities when considering the market imperfections that were not taken into account.

Bhattacharya (1983) conducts an elaborate ex ante vertical spread test using virtually synchronous intraday data from August 1976 through June 1977. He explicitly recognizes the bid-ask spread. If the ISD-range resulting from one option's bid and ask price is disjoint from the ISD-range of another option on the same stock with the same maturity, a vertical spread is implemented (at the respective bid and ask prices). Unlike horizontal spreads, vertical spreads are not flawed by the fact that different volatility estimates across maturities needn't be a bias. To eliminate distortions from early exercise, spreads with likely early exercise according to the pseudo-American formula are eliminated from the sample.

Ex ante, with implementation at the next available trade with nonzero volume after the signal, a surprising average profit of $102.66 per spread is reported.[290] Even

---

[290] See Bhattacharya (1983): op. cit., p. 181. The reported profit is per spread until maturity or until early termination in case of favorable price adjustment.

after fees, the return is still positive. But is it abnormal? The spreads are revised only every two weeks, thus inducing (diversifiable) risk. There is the problem of legging in and legging out. The execution lag is rather short. One should also consider the opportunity costs connected with arbitrage activities. The major impact, however, seems to come from the way the spreads are terminated. The positions are closed early if price adjustments eliminate the mispricing.[291] As in some other tests discussed above, this captures additional profits from favorable price movements that are uncertain at inception. The average profit on profitable spreads is close to $300, while the average loss on unprofitable spreads is $254. This wide dispersion gives an indication of the riskiness of the strategy.

In the face of these shortcomings, the author does not claim that the results are clear proof for market inefficiency.[292]

Chance (1986) implements tests to determine if the pricing bias found in OEX 100 call options can be exploited. The data pertain to the first four months of 1984. To detect mispricings, the at-the-money ISD is used,

---

[291] See ibid. p. 181.

[292] See ibid. p. 183.

and the BS values adjusted for constant dividend yield are computed.

In an intraday ex ante test, calls are bought and sold after an execution lag of no more than 60 minutes and hedged with an appropriate position in the index.[293] The hedge is closed at next day's closing prices. Using a 10% filter for mispricing signals and properly incorporating the bid-ask spread into the prices at which the hedges are established, the average profit per hedge and day is significantly negative at $-11.19.[294]

Also, an intraday ex ante spread test is performed. Overpriced calls are paired with underpriced calls according to the hedge ratios to form a riskless position. The spreads are closed the following day. Again, the average return per spread, using bid-ask data and the 10% mispricing filter, is negative at $-17.07.[295]

Both results strongly suggest market efficiency. Explicit transaction costs don't even need to be taken into account to eliminate apparent profits.[296]

---

293 The author claims that it is conceptually possible to own the index, thus avoiding the detour of using index futures in the test. See p. 150.

294 See Chance (1986): op. cit., p. 161.

295 See ibid. p. 161.

296 See ibid. p. 163-164.

7.4.3. Implications

<u>None</u> of the tests can reject market efficiency by trading on the biases observed in the BS model.[297] This is a strong result, considering that many of the reported profits even incorporated additional returns from favorable price adjustments. Yet, the evidence leaves the question unanswered whether the BS model is the valid and best representative of the option pricing process.

The market imperfections consume most of the apparent returns. Remaining profits can't be proved to be abnormal because of the impossibility to actually implement the positions in a truly riskless manner. While this array of factors seems to eliminate above-normal profit opportunities, the systematic nature of the bias in ISD's remains. Possibly, some other model can better approximate market prices.

Below, two prominent factors ignored in the BS model that might implicitly influence its ISD are discussed. Subsequently, Chapter 8 presents evidence on the relationship between implied and historical stock

[297] As mentioned earlier, a considerable number of trades occur inside the bid-ask spread. Burdening the empirical results with the entire spread might hence understate the achievable after transaction cost returns reported for the tests. However, cost savings from possible trades within the spread are uncertain when the position is about to be established. Also, the efficiency supporting results are fairly robust in most tests, because usually only a fraction of the discussed imperfections and trading impediments has to be considered to eliminate apparent abnormal profits.

volatility and examines further results on the systematic behavior of the ISD's. The findings prompt the discussion of option valuation models that incorporate systematic changes in the variance itself (in contrast to adjusting for ignored factors that might implicitly show up in the ISD).

7.5. Is the Model Incomplete? Implicit Factors that might Cause the Biases

7.5.1. Better Adjustment for Dividends

When the pricing biases in the BS model were found, either the constant dividend yield-adjusted version (e.g. Chance (1986)) or the pseudo-American adjustment (e.g. Macbeth/ Merville (1979), Rubinstein (1985a)) were used. The same is true for most of the trading tests reported above.

The dividend yield-adjusted version assumes that the option will be held to expiration, while the pseudo-American formula reflects either certain early exercise or certain holding to expiration. As already discussed in Chapter 3, both adjustments ignore the opportunity of an American call holder to change his decision about early exercise depending upon the future stock prices at each ex-dividend date. Hence, the true American call value must be higher.

7.5.1.1. The Roll-Geske-Whaley (RGW) formula

For stocks with known dividends, Roll (1977) has solved the valuation of an American call <u>including</u> the effects of early exercise. He shows that its value can be expressed as the value of a portfolio of three European options. Geske (1979b) shows that this portfolio solution can be simplified to a single, but (compared to the BS model) very complex formula. Whaley (1981) corrects errors in both works. The corrected formula is given in appendix 2.

Given the dividend paid is large enough to make early exercise possible (see Subsection 2.1.2.), a prerequisite for this valuation approach is the determination of the ex-dividend stock price S_D above which the call would be exercised early (assuming one dividend payment). This critical stock price can be found in advance by solving the following equation for S_D:[298]

$$c(S_D, t-t_D, K) = S_D+\alpha D-K$$

where t_D is the ex-dividend date, and α is the known decline in the stock price at the ex-dividend date as a proportion of the dividend. (As mentioned before, this factor can be less than one because stocks have been

298 See Roll, Richard: An analytic valuation formula for unprotected American call options on stocks with known dividends, JFEC 5 (1977), pp. 251-258, here p. 254.

observed to decline by less than D due to tax effects.[299] However, this does not influence our discussion.) The bracket (......) contains variables of which c is a function. The ex-dividend stock price S_D, not the cum dividend stock price, is assumed to follow Brownian motion. The dividend is simply added to S_D because it is assumed to be known with certainty.

The intuition behind the equation is that an American call right after the (last) ex-dividend date is worth just as much as a European call. The early exercise feature will then be valueless, assuming all dividend payments are known with certainty. If the value of that European call is lower than the intrinsic value of the American option right before the payment, early exercise is optimal. S_D is the critical stock price where these values are equal. Above it, the cum dividend intrinsic value is higher than the European call value, thus prompting early exercise.

To conclude the introduction of the RGW approach, the portfolio of three European options that gives the holder the same opportunities as an American call is listed below, as corrected by Whaley (1981).[300] (Proof in form of a simple payoff table is given in Roll (1977) and hence

---

[299] See Beckers, Stan: Standard deviations implied in option prices as predictors of future stock price variability, in: Journal of Banking and Finance 5 (1981), pp. 366-381, here p. 366.

[300] See Whaley, Robert E.: On the valuation of American call options on stocks with known dividends, in: JFEC 9 (1981), pp. 207-211, here p. 208.

omitted.)

a) A long position in a European call with exercise price K and maturity t.

b) A long position in a European call with exercise price S_D and maturity an instant before t_D.

c) A short position in a European call on the option in a) with exercise price $S_D+\alpha D-K$ and maturity an instant before t_D. (The valuation of such a compound option has been solved by Geske (1979b) and will be discussed in the context of volatility changes in the next chapter.)

This framework can also be extended to multiple dividend payments.[301]

7.5.1.2. Relation to the BS Biases

Whaley (1981) shows that the RGW value always lies above the pseudo-American value if the stock pays dividends. The pseudo-American formula (though still better than just adjusting the BS value for dividend yield) will hence underprice all American options, including those at the money. When the BS model is "forced" to correctly price at the money options by using their BS model ISD's as a benchmark and then looking for

---

[301] See Roll (1977): op. cit., p. 257; or Geske, Robert: A note on an analytical valuation formula for unprotected American call options on stocks with known dividends, in: JFEC 7 (1979a), pp. 375-380, here p. 377.

biases, this procedure will be a cause for those very biases. It thus warrants closer examination.

Geske and Roll (1984) contrast pseudo-American values with RGW values. For one dividend payment before expiration, the pseudo-American value can be plotted as two branches. One assumes certain early exercise. Written as a function of the relevant variables, the (European) value of the call in the early exercise branch is hence $c_{ex}(S_{cum}, t_\epsilon, K)$, where t_ϵ is an instant before the ex-dividend date. The other branch assumes holding to maturity with certainty. Its value is hence $c_{hold}(S_{cum}-PV(D), t, K)$.

Early exercise is more likely for in-the-money-options and less likely for out-of-the-money options. Consequently, c_{hold} lies above c_{ex} for out-of-the-money options and below c_{ex} for in-the-money options. The two branches intersect near the money.[302]

Consider a test of the striking price bias where we ignore early exercise: we assume all options are held to expiration, hence valuing them with c_{hold}. Consequently, c_{hold} is forced to equal the observed American value (which here is represented by RGW) for at-the-money options,

---

[302] See Geske, Robert / Roll, Richard: On valuing American call options with the Black-Scholes European formula, in: JOF 39 (1984), pp. 443-455, here p. 449. The authors do not elaborate on factors that might affect the exact position of the intersection. I would like to point out that the intersection should move further into the money the higher the volatility, the lower the dividend, and the earlier it is paid, because this will raise the value alive and lower the benefit from early exercise.

because c_{hold} is employed to determine the benchmark ISD. This yields an overstated estimate for the true implied stock volatility (recall that RGW always lies above the two branches).

Geske and Roll (1984) show that c_{hold} as a function of K has a different slope than RGW. RGW decreases more with rising striking price than c_{hold}. When c_{hold} is forced to equal RGW for at-the-money options, c_{hold} will thus be <u>above</u> RGW for out-of-the-money options and <u>below</u> RGW for in-the-money options when the at-the-money volatility is used to compute all the c_{hold} values. This relationship is shown in the figure below.

Figure 7.a.: RGW Values vs. c_{hold} when c_{hold} is computed with the at-the-money ISD

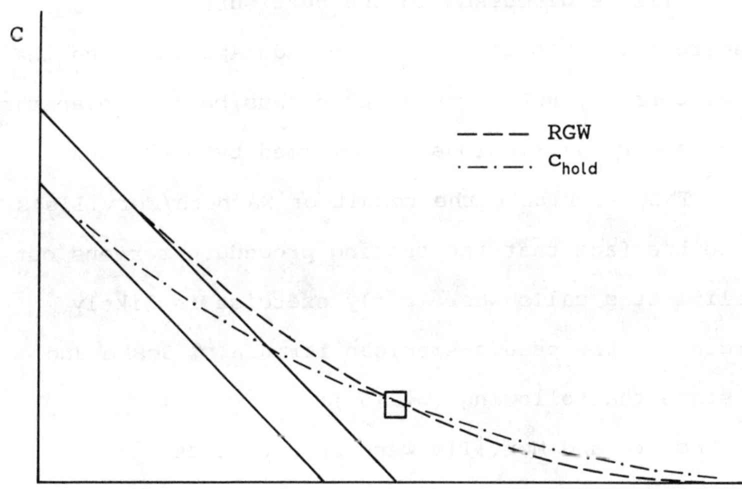

(from: Geske and Roll (1984), p. 450)

Consequently, if RGW represents the correct valuation method for traded American options, the ISD's implied by c_{hold} for them will be <u>lower</u> for out-of-the-money options and <u>higher</u> for in-the-money options, i.e. the BS model will be found to overprice out-of-the-money options and underprice in-the-money options.

This bias is exactly the one found by Macbeth and Merville (1979), Chance (1986), and in Rubinstein's (1985) first period. The reverse bias reported by Black (1975) and in Rubinstein's (1985) second period can be explained if certain early exercise is assumed by employing c_{ex} to value the options, because c_{ex} displays the opposite behavior of c_{hold}. Whether c_{ex} was really employed in these 2 tests will be discussed in the next subsection.

The relationship between the pseudo-American and the (deemed correct) RGW formula could thus be an explanation for the empirical findings, as claimed by Geske and Roll.[303] They attribute the result of Macbeth/Merville's test to the fact that the testing procedure screens out and eliminates calls where early exercise is likely according to the pseudo-American formula.[304] Geske and Roll state the following (p. 450):

"When Macbeth and Merville were able to detect a

---

[303]See ibid. p. 454.

[304]See Macbeth/Merville (1979): op. cit., p. 1182.

significant probability of early exercise, they eliminated that option from the sample. Thus, they were more likely to have found the ..... (in-the-money underpricing) bias, which they indeed did find."

In various additional comments throughout their paper, the authors blame this elimination procedure for the bias.

I will now show that this claim is incorrect. On the contrary, the screening should mitigate (although not entirely eliminate) the dividend-induced bias. If options with likely early exercise according to the pseudo-American formula are screened out, this is equivalent to eliminating all cases where c_{hold} is below c_{ex}. This will in particular be the case for deep-in-the-money options (recall that the branches intersect near-the-money). Consequently, out-of-the-money and at-the-money calls on dividend-paying stocks will be valued according to the c_{hold} branch, which lies (as pointed out above) below RGW. However, if the screening procedure is perfectly accurate, in-the-money calls on dividend paying stocks will not be contained in the sample if their early exercise seems optimal (c_{ex} would be higher than c_{hold}). Most deep-in-the-money calls that remain will therefore be those on nondividend-paying stocks. However, their c_{hold} value is the same as their BS value without dividends and will be equal to the RGW value (because the value of American options, or for that matter RGW value, is equal to the European value if the stock doesn't pay dividends).

In summary, the sample will consequently contain out-of-the-money and at-the-money calls where the screening doesn't have any mitigating effect, but it will not contain any in-the-money options that are grossly undervalued by c_{hold} where early exercise is ignored. In addition, the fraction of options in the sample where no dividend is paid before maturity, thus being valued equal to RGW, is higher. Taken together, the c_{hold} values for the sample options will on average still lie below RGW and still display essentially the same slope discrepancy and hence the same pricing bias that was discussed. But this discrepancy should be substantially smaller, not higher as claimed by Geske and Roll (1984).

Rubinstein (1985a) uses the same screening procedure for his sample. Chance (1986) does not screen out options with likely early exercise. Yet, he is able to justify this by showing that an adjustment for continuous dividend yield (which is in essence equivalent to using c_{hold}) for the entire sample is appropriate, because the dispersion of dividend payments on the stocks in the index that underlies the OEX 100 option virtually rules out optimal early exercise.[305]

In summary, the early exercise effect can cause the in-the-money underpricing / out-of-the-money overpricing bias if c_{hold} is used, even after screening. Yet, this very screening should substantially alleviate the bias. Hence, it is doubtful whether the RGW formula can really explain the entire magnitude of the deviations. This will be addressed in the next subsection.

Geske and Roll (1984) claim that undervaluation by the BS model of close to maturity options (the time to expiration bias) can also be attributed to the selection procedure described above. Close to maturity, a sample where c_{ex} is screened out will consist of 2 types of options: For one, there will be options where no more dividend payment is expected, and that therefore don't cause any bias when valued with the BS model. The second type are those options where a dividend payment is still awaited, and whose BS value will hence be c_{hold} if c_{ex} is screened out. Since c_{hold} is below RGW, these type 2 options will cause the computed implied volatility for short maturity options to be higher, i.e. the BS model

305 See Chance (1986): op. cit., pp. 144-145.

underprices them.[306] Combined with the striking price bias connected with c_{hold}, this will be most severe for in-the-money options.[307]

However, the authors ignore that the composition of the sample will be exactly the same for longer maturity options as well.

7.5.1.3. Evidence on the Dividend Effect and the Empirical Performance of the RGW formula

Geske and Roll (1984) provide evidence that the dividend yield and the interest rate tend to move together. They also conclude that a higher level of dividends dominates the call value raising effect of higher interest rates (see Chapter 3) as far as optimal early exercise is concerned.[308]

Consequently, if both c_{hold} and c_{ex} are left in the sample (i.e. the option value is determined with both branches of the pseudo-American formula), c_{ex} will mainly determine the pseudo-American value when dividends (and interest rates) are high, and c_{hold} when they are low. Comparing concurrent dividend yields and interest rates with the striking price bias tests of Macbeth/Merville

---

[306] See Geske/Roll (1984): op. cit., p. 452.

[307] See ibid. p. 452.

[308] See ibid. p. 446.

(1979) and Rubinstein (1985a) reveals that they seem to conform to this line of reasoning. The bias pertaining to c_{hold} (in-the-money underpricing, out-of-the-money overpricing) prevailed when yields were low, and the reverse bias pertaining to c_{ex} (Rubinstein's second period) prevailed when yields were high.[309]

However, Geske and Roll's linking of the bias to c_{ex} and c_{hold} is not very convincing. The two tests examined discarded c_{ex} from their sample, thus making it impossible to charge c_{ex} with the bias reversal. For a subsample consisting of calls without ex-dividend dates, Rubinstein (1985a) confirms the persistence of the bias as well as its reversal from his first to his second examination period (although some alleviating effects are apparent compared to the sample where dividends are paid).[310] Since the American value equals the (European) BS value if no dividends are paid, this finding shows that the RGW formula is unlikely to capture everything.

Sterk (1983a) investigates relationships between the striking price bias and the level of dividends paid on the underlying stocks. He uses both the RGW and the pseudo-American formula. Unexpectedly, both models display the

---

[309] See ibid. pp. 446-447.

[310] See Rubinstein (1985): op. cit., p. 478.

same bias, and surprisingly, the relationship to the dividend level is exactly opposite to the arguments in Geske/Roll (1984): In-the-money (out-of-the-money) calls on stocks with low dividends are overpriced, and this bias reverses when dividends are high.[311] The results are robust and persist even when differences in ISD and the time to expiration of the options in the sample are taken into account.

In another test, Sterk (1983b) compares the relative performance of the RGW and pseudo-American formulas. The pseudo-American approximation can be expected to perform reasonably well when early exercise is either very likely or very unlikely, because its two branches (for one dividend payment) assume either certain early exercise or certain holding to expiration. Early exercise is less likely (more likely) if the option is out-of-the-money (in-the-money), and naturally, the size of the dividend plays a substantial role.

When early exercise is either likely or unlikely according to these factors, the RGW model is not significantly better in the test. But in the range in between, it shows superior performance.[312] It should be

---

[311] See Sterk, William E.: Option pricing: dividends and the in- and out-of-the-money bias, in: FM (Winter 1983a), pp. 47-53, here p. 49.

[312] See Sterk, William E.: Comparative performance of the Black-Scholes and Roll-Geske-Whaley option pricing models, in: JFQA 18 (1983b), pp. 345-354, here p. 353.

noted that all new options are issued at-the-money and are thus likely to be in that range.

In conclusion, the evidence on the performance of the RGW model is equivocal. While it all in all apparently works better than the BS pseudo-American formula when dividends have to be considered, it cannot solve the "mystery" of the pricing biases. At best, it alleviates them. Given its complexity, it hence would be surprising if the RGW model were to replace the pseudo-American adjustment as a widely used method.

7.5.2. Tax Effects

The taxation of options has been addressed in Chapter 4. Recall that the hedge ratio was found to be influenced by taxes if covered calls are written. It will now be shown that this affects the call price at which a covered writer is willing to sell his option.

Without taxation, the number of options written to hedge one share long is $1/N(d_1)$. For a short time period Δt, the change in the equity value I of the hedge is thus:

$$\Delta I = \Delta S - \frac{1}{N(d_1)} \Delta C$$

To rule out any confusion: in this subsection, Δ denotes a

variable change in a time interval.

If the writer plans to hold on to his initial stock position indefinitely, gains and losses on it will remain unrealized and hence untaxed. However, the writer will realize capital gains on the options when buying them back at a lower price or letting them expire. Conversely, he will realize tax deductible losses when buying them back at a higher price or when buying additional stock to deliver if the call is exercised against him (see Section 4.8.). This taxation or deduction thus proportionally reduces the gains and losses in the option part of the hedge:[313]

$$\Delta I = \Delta S - \frac{1}{N(d_1)} \Delta C(1-x)$$

where x is the ordinary income tax rate. Since the Government assumes x of the value change or risk of the written option, the position is not a perfect hedge any more. In order to cancel out the tax effect, the hedge ratio must be amended appropriately to $\frac{1}{N(d_1)(1-x)}$, thus requiring more options to be written per share long to

[313] See Scholes (1976): op. cit., p. 321.
Comment: This line of reasoning obviously relies on the assumption that the investor has positive taxable income from which capital losses can be deducted.

compensate for the risk reduction:[314]

$$\Delta I = \Delta S - \frac{1}{N(d_1)(1-x)} * \Delta C(1-x)$$

In equilibrium, the equity

$$I = S - \frac{1}{N(d_1)(1-x)} C$$

in the hedge position should earn the riskless after tax rate of interest over every revision interval ($e^{r\Delta t(1-x)}-1$). Scholes (1976) shows that this relationship yields the same solution as the BS model adjusted for constant dividend yield, where rx is now equivalent to that dividend yield:

$$C = Se^{-rxt}N(d_1) - Ke^{-rt}N(d_2)$$

This result has an important implication: if all calls were written by covered writers with indefinitely held stock positions, call values would be systematically <u>lower</u> than in a no-tax world.

On the other hand, tax-free market participants such as pension funds or trusts would be willing to pay the normal BS value. The same is true for dealers and market makers trading in options and stocks. Since they usually don't hold positions indefinitely, they realize all gains and

---

[314] See ibid. p. 322.
Comment: As will become obvious from the valuation formula presented shortly, $N(d_1)$ in the tax-adjusted hedge must differ from the original BS hedge ratio (see Subsection 3.2.1.): for its computation, S is replaced by Se^{-rxt}.

losses on both options and stocks, which cancels out the tax effects.[315]

Consequently, covered taxable writers have an incentive to write options at the regular BS value, while option buyers would be glad to buy at the lower tax-adjusted value. In particular, buyers in high tax brackets would pay less than those in low tax brackets (or dealers), because one can alternatively replicate the call with an indefinite long position in stocks and borrowing, thus getting tax deduction on the interest paid.

Hence, high tax bracket investors have an incentive to write covered calls, while low tax bracket investors have an incentive to buy them: if the tax effects are shared between the two groups, with observed prices lying in between, both can gain at the expense of the Government, and an explanation for biases where the BS model overprices options can be given.[316]

Heaton (1986) tests the interest rate implied in option prices. He argues that this rate should reflect the after tax borrowing rate of the marginal investor who is indifferent between holding the option or replicating it. He finds that the implied interest rate is less than the

---

[315] See ibid. p. 323.

[316] See ibid. p. 327.

pre-tax T-bill rate. This in turn implies that option prices in the market are lower than the no-tax values, conforming to a tax bracket at the upper end of the progression for private borrowers who borrow at the typical margin account rate.[317]

The result confirms the effects and incentives discussed above. The tax effect also provides a rationale for often cited empirical observations that find deep-in-the-money calls frequently trading at intrinsic value (i.e. heavy overpricing by the BS model).[318]

Do these results give rise to "permanent" arbitrage opportunities? In theory, low tax investors could borrow cheaply by buying the calls and shorting the stock, and then make arbitrage profits by lending the proceeds. The opposite strategy applies to high tax bracket investors. However, the high transaction costs involved in rebalancing the hedge, as well as short sale restrictions, are likely to eliminate any profit opportunities.[319]

It should be noted that the tax effect can explain only overpricing by the BS model. It is therefore incapable of explaining the entire array of pricing biases and their reversals that have been discussed.

---

[317] See Heaton, Hal: Options and tax clienteles, in: Advances in Futures and Options Research, Volume 1, Part A (1986), pp. 167-179, here p. 176.

[318] See Black (1975): op. cit., p. 64; Scholes (1976): op. cit., p. 327.

[319] See Heaton (1986): op. cit., p. 177.

8. EXPLICIT INCORPORATION OF VOLATILITY CHANGES

Instead of trying to recognize factors that might implicitly alter an otherwise correct and stable stock volatility implied in option prices, one can develop alternative models that explicitly incorporate a particular behavior of the volatility. Unlike adjustments for implicit factors that were discussed above, this approach can also capture systematic changes in the stock volatility itself, allowing an explicit departure from the stationarity assumption.

Chapter 4 has presented evidence on nonstationary variance. Empirical tests have been performed that contrast historical stock price behavior with ISD's implied in the Black-Scholes model. They reveal that the behavior of ISD's can provide useful insights into changes in the market's assessment of future stock volatility. Consequently, findings in this context are discussed next. Thereafter, the relationship between systematic changes in stock volatility and the Black-Scholes pricing bias they imply is presented. A discussion of various models that incorporate such relationships follows. The chapter concludes with empirical evidence on the performance of those models.

8.1. The Performance and Behavior of Implied Volatility as a Predictor of Future Stock Price Volatility

So far, we have employed ISD's merely as a measure of pricing bias. However, the ISD also represents the market's expectation of future stock volatility. Its behavior hence reflects possible systematic changes in those expectations, thus warranting a closer look.

Latané and Rendleman (1976) compute a weighted average ISD (with the calls' Lambdas as weights) and regress it on the actual stock price volatility that is subsequently realized. The results are compared to the predictive performance of historical stock price volatility, measured over the preceding four years. The findings show that the weighted ISD is a far better predictor of future volatility than the historical data (correlation of .826 versus .686).[320]

Interestingly, there is also a strong tendency for the ISD's to move together over time, i.e. the weighted ISD's of the options on all stocks in the sample decrease or increase together. For one, this result is further evidence for the notion that the variance is nonstationary. Secondly, it also shows that investors may

---

[320] See Latané/Rendleman (1976): op. cit., p. 376.

alter their assessment of the riskiness of stocks in general. This indicates that factors not captured as variables in the BS model, for example macroeconomic variables that don't have anything to do with the specific underlying stock, may systematically influence all option prices indirectly through the volatility variable.

Beckers (1981) contrasts weighting schemes for the ISD with the predictive performance of the ISD for at-the-money options, which (as noted before) are the most sensitive to volatility changes (highest Λ). His sample consists of daily CBOE and NYSE closing prices from April 1975 through October 1977.

All ISD measures are found to outperform historical volatility measures. In addition, the at-the-money ISD outperforms the weighted measures. This result confirms the previously mentioned notion that the BS model works best for at-the-money options, and that the at-the-money ISD should hence be the best benchmark when looking for pricing biases.[321]

Again, the volatility is found to be nonstationary. The ISD's fluctuate from day to day and again tend to move

[321] See Beckers, Stan: Standard deviations implied in option prices as predictors of future stock price variability, in: Journal of Banking and Finance 5 (1981), pp. 366-381, here p. 376.

together.[322]

Schmalensee and Trippi (1978) use weekly data to investigate what might cause the ISD's to change. Their sample is taken from the period between April 1974 and May 1975. They, too, confirm that ISD's change through time and tend to move together.

Surprisingly, the authors find very little evidence that the magnitude of the underlying stock's movement during the week (as a measure reflecting the latest historical volatility) would affect its option's ISD at the end of the week. Also, the magnitude of the past week's fluctuations in the stock market as a whole, represented by the S&P 500 index, does not have any effect, and the influence of the direction of those market movements does not exhibit any consistent pattern.[323]

However, there is a striking effect related to the direction of movements in the underlying stock: increases in the stock price decrease its volatility.[324] This corroborates the findings of Beckers (1980) and Christie (1982) that were discussed in Section 4.1., who attribute this behavior to the influence of leverage.

---

[322]See ibid. p. 370 and 377.

[323]See Schmalensee, Richard / Trippi, Robert R.: Common stock volatility expectations implied by option premia, in: JOF 33 (1978), pp. 129-147, here p. 140 and 144.

[324]See ibid. p. 139.

It is important to note that Schmalensee and Trippi find the tendency of ISD's to move together to persist even after the effects of stock price increases or decreases are filtered out.[325] This again hints at the possible influence of macroeconomic variables unrelated to the stock price behavior.

The superior predictive performance of ISD's is confirmed in the tests discussed above. This indicates that their behavior should provide useful information for the analysis of the option pricing process in the market. The implications of the evidence presented above on this behavior are twofold:

On the one hand, there seem to be relationships between increases or decreases in the stock price and changes in its volatility. Therefore, the effects of such relationships on the distribution of stock prices is addressed next. Subsequently, their incorporation into option valuation models will be discussed.

On the other hand, the tendency of IDS's to move together can only be explained by marketwide changes in volatility expectations that are unrelated to stock price movements.[326] Hence, one cannot expect these models to

---

[325] See ibid. p. 141.

[326] See ibid. p. 141.

capture everything.

8.2. <u>The Effects of Systematic Volatility Changes on the Stock Price Distribution</u>

Systematic relationships between stock price increases or decreases and the volatility cause systematic deviations from lognormality. They thus also cause deviations from the Brownian motion that describes the stock price movement in the Black-Scholes derivation. The figures below show three situations where the terminal stock price distribution departs from lognormality:

Figure 8.a.: $\rho<0$,
left tail fatter

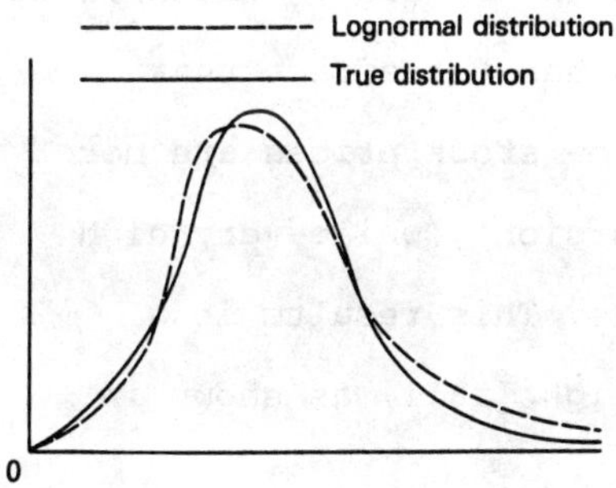

Figure 8.b.: $\rho>0$,
right tail fatter

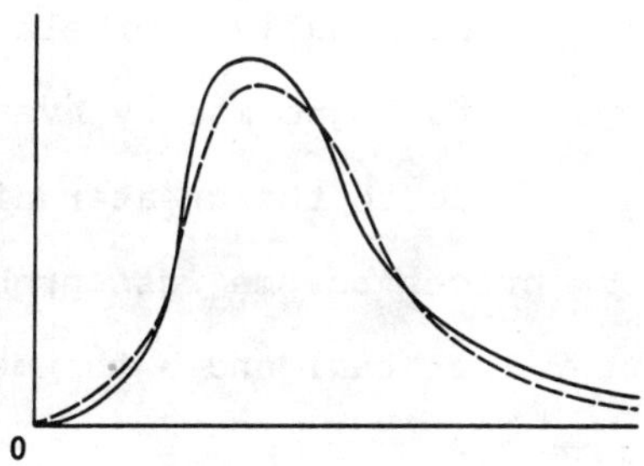

(from: Hull, John C.: Options, Futures and other Derivative Securities, Englewood Cliffs 1989, p. 306.)

Figure 8.c.: Both tails fatter

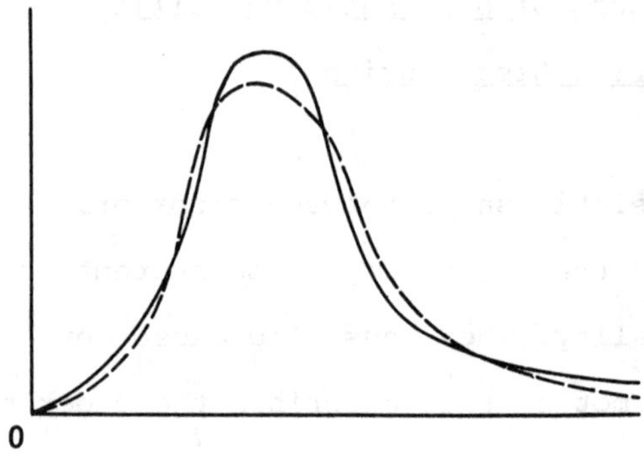

(from Hull, John C.: Options, Futures and other Derivative Securities, Englewood Cliffs 1989, p. 306.)

If the volatility is negatively correlated with the stock price ($\rho<0$), the volatility will rise when the stock price declines. This is the relationship found by Schmalensee and Trippi (1978), Beckers (1980) and Christie (1982). The negative correlation has the effect that compared to lognormality, very low stock prices are more likely (due to the greater dispersion), while very high stock prices become less probable. This results in a fatter left tail and a thinner right tail, as shown in Figure 8.a.

Conversely, if volatility and stock price are positively correlated ($\rho>0$), the volatility will rise when the stock price rises. This implies that very high stock prices are more likely, and very low stock prices are less likely. The result is a thinner left tail and a fatter right tail of the stock price distribution, thus conforming to Figure 8.b.

If large movements in the stock price in either direction cause increases in the volatility, both tails are fatter. This conforms to Figure 8.c.[327]

Each of these relationships results in a different BS bias. An out-of-the-money call will have positive value at expiration only if there is a significant increase in the stock price. Its value therefore depends on the right tail of the stock price distribution. The fatter this tail, the higher the option value.[328] Therefore, the BS model will underprice out-of-the-money calls in Figure 8.b. and 8.c., and overprice them in Figure 8.a.

Equivalently, an out-of-the-money put depends on the left tail of the stock price distribution. The fatter this tail is, the more valuable the put is. Hence, the BS model will underprice out-of-the-money puts in Figure 8.a. and 8.c., and overprice them in Figure 8.b.

The biases for in-the-money options can be determined

---

[327] Fat tails for the lognormal stock price distribution are not directly inferable from the leptokurtic distribution of stock return logarithms that was presented in Subsection 4.1.2.

[328] See Hull: Options, op. cit., p. 307.

by using the put-call parity, which is independent of the terminal stock price distribution. For the purposes of our discussion, the European version (which ignores early exercise) is sufficient:

$$p+S = c+Ke^{-rt}$$

If the call is in the money, the corresponding put is out of the money, and vice versa. Therefore, to uphold the parity, in-the-money calls must exhibit the same bias as out-of-the-money puts, and vice versa.[329] Consequently, the BS model will underprice in-the-money calls in Figure 8.a. and 8.c., and overprice them in figure 8.b.

8.3. Alternative Models that Incorporate Volatility Changes

Option valuation models can capture the biases by establishing a relationship between stock price movements and the volatility. Also, models where the stock price exhibits jumps (in contrast to the continuous tiny changes in Black/Scholes underlying Brownian motion) can result in distributions that deviate from lognormality.

The models presented below will hence under- or overprice options compared to the BS values and can thus serve to alleviate the striking price biases corresponding

---

[329] See ibid. p. 307.

to the figures above. The details of their derivation are not the focus of their discussion. Rather, the intuition behind the respective model concept and the resulting departure from lognormality is pointed out. Subsection 8.4. subsequently presents evidence on the empirical performance of the models.

8.3.1. The Compound Option Model

The equity of a levered firm can be viewed as a call option on the value of the firm. If F is the face value of the outstanding debt, and V the value of the firm, then the total value of the equity at maturity of the debt will be max [0, V^*-F]. The sum of the stock prices is the market value of the firm's equity. A call on the stock that expires earlier than the debt is hence an option on an option, a so-called compound option.

Geske (1979) has solved the valuation of such an option. If the value of the entire firm (not just the stock) is assumed to follow Brownian motion, then the volatility of the stock, σ_s, is shown to be related to the (constant) volatility of the firm, σ_V, in the following manner:[330]

[330] See Geske, Robert: The valuation of compound options, in: JFEC 7 (1979a), pp. 63-81, here p. 69.

$$\sigma_S = \frac{\partial S}{\partial V} * \frac{V}{S}\sigma_V$$

Therefore, since $\frac{\partial S}{\partial V} > 0$:

$$\frac{\partial \sigma_S}{\partial S} = -\frac{V}{S^2}\left(\frac{\partial S}{\partial V}\right)\sigma_V < 0$$

This means that the stock volatility rises when the stock price falls. Hence, the compound option formula incorporates the leverage effect and captures the bias conforming to Figure 8.a. The formula is given in appendix 3.

8.3.2. The Constant Elasticity of Variance (CEV) Model

Let us assume that the debt D of a firm is riskless, implying that the debt's value is not influenced at all by changes in leverage. In such an environment, $\frac{\partial S}{\partial V} = 1$, i.e. the stock (or equity) value S moves perfectly with the firm value V. Consequently, the relationship between σ_S and σ_V introduced above transforms to:

$$\sigma_S = 1 * \frac{V}{S}\sigma_V = \frac{D+S}{S}\sigma_V = \left(1 + \frac{D}{S}\right)\sigma_V$$

Thus, the elasticity ϵ of the stock volatility σ_S with respect to the stock price is:[331]

$$\epsilon = \frac{\left(\frac{\partial \sigma_s}{\sigma_s}\right)}{\left(\frac{\partial S}{S}\right)} = -\frac{D}{D+S}, \quad \text{and} \quad -1 \leq \epsilon \leq 0$$

It can be shown that even with risky debt, the range of the elasticity is still bounded by [-1,0].[332] The formula above shows that $\epsilon=0$ when there is no debt at all, and ϵ approaches -1 when the firm is virtually entirely financed with debt.

Cox and Ross (1976) have solved the option valuation problem for the case where ϵ is a constant within that range. More precisely, the elasticity of the stock <u>variance</u> which can be shown to be simply 2ϵ,[333] is assumed constant. For the CEV diffusion process, the instantaneous volatility of the CCRR in continuous time is given as:

$$\sigma S^{\frac{(\alpha-2)}{2}}$$

where σ is the volatility in Brownian motion that corresponds to the Black/Scholes lognormal distribution

---

331 See Christie (1982): op. cit., p. 408.

332 See ibid. p. 408.

333 See ibid. p. 408.

(when $\alpha=2$), and $2 \geq \alpha \geq 0$.[334] Over finite time intervals, $\epsilon=0$ corresponds to $\alpha=2$, and $\epsilon=-1$ corresponds to $\alpha=0$. Hence, the range $[-1,0]$ for ϵ is recognized in the above process.

For $\alpha=2$ (or $\epsilon=0$), the instantaneous volatility is σ, i.e. the CEV diffusion process corresponds to the BS model in this particular case.[335] For $\alpha=0$ (or $\epsilon=-1$), the instantaneous volatility is inversely proportional to the stock price: σS^{-1}. This case is called the absolute diffusion model, and its formula is given in appendix 3.[336] (The general CEV formulas are very complex, and hence their reproduction in this thesis is omitted).

The CEV model accords to the same line of reasoning as the compound option model: increasing leverage increases the volatility. Leverage can be financial leverage (debt), but it can also be operating leverage (fixed costs). It rises when the stock price falls, and hence the volatility rises when the stock price falls, thus capturing the bias in Figure 8.a.[337] The only exception is the limiting case where $\epsilon=0$ and the CEV model collapses to the BS model.

---

[334] See Beckers (1980): op. cit., p. 662.

[335] See Macbeth, James D. / Merville, Larry J.: Tests of the Black-Scholes and Cox call option valuation models, in: JOF 35 (1980), pp. 285-301, here p. 287.

[336] See Beckers (1980): op. cit., p. 666.

[337] See Hull: Options, op. cit., p. 311.

Under the CEV point of view, the BS model is therefore adequate for firms without leverage.

A weak aspect of the CEV model is that it ignores that ϵ changes, too, when the leverage changes (see equation above).[338] Therefore, the requirement that ϵ be constant does not capture the entire relationship between leverage and volatility.

8.3.3. The Displaced Diffusion Model

Rubinstein (1983) has developed the so-called displaced diffusion model. The firm is assumed to hold two types of assets: risky assets, with a constant volatility, and riskless assets that provide the riskless return e^{rt}. Also, there is assumed to be a fixed amount of default-free (i.e. riskless) debt. The model's key parameter, a, is defined as:

$$a = \alpha(1+\beta)$$

where α denotes the initial risky fraction of the firm's total assets, and β is the debt-to-equity ratio $(\frac{D}{S})$.[339] (When dividends are incorporated, the parameter becomes more complex.)

---

338 See Christie (1982): op. cit., p. 423+429.

339 See Rubinstein, Mark: Displaced diffusion option pricing, in: JOF 38 (1983), pp.213-217, here p. 215.

When a>1, the firm has less riskless assets than debt. When netting off the riskless assets against the debt, one is left with the risky assets and the remaining (assumed riskless) debt. The resulting model is similar to the compound option model described above and hence captures the bias in Figure 8.a. Its weakness (unlike the compound option model) is the failure to take default on the debt into account. If the face value of the debt exceeds the total value of all assets, the model assumes negative equity value.[340]

When a<1, there is less riskless debt than riskless assets. Netting off the debt against the riskless assets yields the following composition of the remaining equity:

$$S = S_{risk} + S_{rl}$$

where S is the value of equity, S_{risk} is the value of the risky assets, and S_{rl} the value of net riskless assets. Since S_{rl} is riskless, its return does not exhibit any volatility. Except for a certain upward drift in S_{rl} that must equal the riskless interest rate, any movement in S is therefore entirely determined by S_{risk}. S increases when S_{risk} increases. Since risky assets then become a larger part of S (if the S_{risk} increase is larger than the upward drift in S_{rl}), the volatility of the stock also increases. The reverse is true when the stock price declines. This

---

[340] See Hull: Options, op. cit., p. 310.

will be entirely due to declining S_{risk}, resulting in the risky fraction to become smaller and hence decreasing the stock volatility.[341] Consequently, volatility and stock price are positively correlated for a<1, and the model captures the bias in Figure 8.b.

The formula for the displaced diffusion model is given in appendix 3.

8.3.4. The Pure Jump Model

The pure jump model is elaborated on in Cox/Ross/Rubinstein (1979). In each small time interval Δt, the stock price S declines to $Se^{-w\Delta t}$ with probability $1-\gamma\Delta t$, where w is the rate of decline. Occasionally, it exhibits jumps from S to uS with probability $\gamma\Delta t$, where u>1. Note that this jump probability approaches zero when the time increment Δt gets very small.[342]

In the limit, when $\Delta t \to 0$, the jumps occur according to a poisson process at rate γ. The resulting stock price distribution after finite intervals is log-poisson. The pure jump model corresponds to Figure 8.b., i.e. the volatility is positively correlated with the stock

[341] See Rubinstein (1983): op. cit., p. 215; Hull: Options: op. cit., p. 310.

[342] See Cox/Ross/Rubinstein (1979): op. cit., p. 254.

price.[343]

The formula can be found in appendix 3. The model's unrealistic feature is that jumps are assumed to be only positive.

8.3.5. The Jump Diffusion Model

The jump diffusion model was developed by Merton (1976). It suggests a stock price movement where jumps are superimposed upon geometric Brownian motion. The jumps are assumed to be triggered by extraordinary new information (e.g. some important announcement) that has more than just a marginal impact on the stock price and hence moves it far more than the "normal" vibrations modeled by Brownian motion. (These are jumps in continuous time, as addressed in Chapter 4.2.) The probability of these significant information arrivals is drawn from a poisson distribution, where γ is the arrival rate.[344]

The magnitude of the jumps as a proportional change in the stock price is a random variable with an expected value of k. The average stock price growth rate that is caused by jumps is γk. Hence, the expected instantaneous

---

[343] See Hull: Options, op. cit., p. 312.

[344] See Merton, Robert C.: Option pricing when underlying stock returns are discontinuous, in: JFEC 3 (1976), pp. 125-144, here pp. 127-128.

growth rate in the Brownian motion is changed from μ to $\mu-\gamma k$.[345] These specifications for the stock's movement result in a sample path that is continuous most of the time (from the Brownian motion), with finite jumps of differing sign and magnitude occurring at discrete points in time.[346]

The key assumption on which the model relies is that the jumps constitute nonsystematic (diversifiable) risk, i.e. they are uncorrelated with the market. This could be the case if the extraordinary information that causes jumps is firm specific (e.g. announcement of an important invention or discovery). Therefore, a BS type hedge portfolio that eliminates the risk from the continuous component in the stock's movement should still yield the riskless rate of return. This line of reasoning makes it possible to derive a valuation formula (which is given in appendix 3), although it is obviously doubtful that there should not be any extraordinary information that affects all stock prices together. (Recall, for example, the evidence that ISD's move together.)

It must be pointed out that in spite of the assumed nonsystematic character of the jump risk in this model, the jumps do affect the option price, i.e. one cannot

---

[345] See Hull: Options, op. cit., p. 313.

[346] See Merton (1976): op. cit., p. 129.

simply ignore them.[347] The jumps result in fatter tails compared to the lognormal distribution. Consequently, the model captures the bias in Figure 8.c., where the BS model underprices both in-the-money and out-of-the-money options.[348] When $\gamma=0$ (i.e. no jumps), the jump diffusion model reduces to the BS formula.

8.3.6. The Stochastic Volatility Model

Hull and White (1988) consider the case where the variance of the stock is a random variable. Its movement is assumed to be governed by a process similar to the Brownian motion of the stock price. This induces deviations from BS values.

The nonstochastic component (drift) of changes in the variance is manipulated in order to allow investigation of the effects caused by three particular types of movement in the variance:

1. The variance is stochastic and reverts slowly to its long-run average level.
2. The variance is stochastic and reverts quickly to its long-run average level.
3. The variance is stochastic and has no drift component.

---

[347] See ibid. pp. 133-134.

[348] See ibid. p. 140.

In addition, each of these types of movement in the variance can be linked with the stock price by assuming positive, negative or zero correlation.[349] Yet, the resulting deviations from BS values have the same direction for all three types of variance movement. Only the deviation magnitude differs.

Assuming zero correlation with the stock price, the option value can be shown to equal the BS value, integrated over the distribution of the mean volatility over the life of the option. This captures the bias in Figure 8.c.[350]

When the correlation is positive or negative, there is no closed-form solution for the option value. Hull and White (1988) determine the values by means of a series solution and Monte Carlo simulation. For negative correlation between the volatility and the stock price, the model captures the bias in Figure 8.a. For positive correlation, it corresponds to Figure 8.b.[351]

A somewhat surprising result of the simulations is that for reasonable values of the parameters involved in the model, the deviations from the corresponding BS price are

---

[349] See Hull, John / White, Alan: An analysis of the bias in option pricing cause by a stochastic volatility, in: Advances in Futures and Options Research, Volume 3 (1988), pp. 29-61, here p. 32 and pp. 38-40.

[350] See Hull: Options, op. cit., p. 315.

[351] See Hull/White (1988): op. cit., p. 44.

relatively small. Except for deep-out-of-the-money options, the stochastic volatility causes deviations of less than 5%.[352]

8.3.7. A Summarizing Categorization

In order to summarize and contrast the properties of the models introduced above, the following table categorizes them according to the striking price bias they capture:

<u>Figure 8.a.</u>: BS model underprices in-the-money calls and overprices out-of-the-money calls	* compound option model * CEV model * displaced diffusion model when a>1 * stochastic volatility model when stock price and volatility are negatively correlated
<u>Figure 8.b.</u>: BS model overprices in-the-money calls and underprices out-of-the-money calls	* displaced diffusion model when a<1 * pure jump model * stochastic volatility model when stock price and volatility are negatively correlated
<u>Figure 8.c.</u>: BS model underprices both in- and out-of-the-money calls	* jump diffusion model * stochastic volatility model when stock price and volatility have zero correlation

352 See Hull: Options, op. cit., p. 314.

8.4. Empirical Evidence on the Performance of the Models

Beckers (1980) supports the validity of the CEV model because his sample of stock returns, taken from Sept.1972 through Sept.1977, mostly exhibits a negative correlation between volatility and stock prices.[353]

Macbeth and Merville (1980) directly compare the performance of the CEV model with the BS formula, using data for the year 1976. They find the CEV prices closer to market prices on virtually every trading day for the options on all six stocks that are examined. However, the CEV model does not deliver a perfect fit, either.[354]

While the authors above explicitly address the CEV model, their results implicitly support the other models that capture the striking price bias in Figure 8.a. as well (BS underpricing of in-the-money call options, overpricing of out-of-the-money call options).

Rubinstein (1985a) considers which option valuation models could explain the striking price biases found in his sample of option prices. Recall from Chapter 7.1. that he finds the BS model to underprice in-the-money calls and overprice out-of-the-money calls in the period between

---

[353] See Beckers (1980): op. cit., p. 663.

[354] See Macbeth/Merville (1980): op. cit., p. 291.

August 1976 and Oct.21, 1977. But thereafter, until the end of his sample period, in August 1978, the bias is reversed (Figure 8.b.).

Rubinstein examines the ability of five of the six models discussed above in section 8.3. to explain these biases. In particular, the compound option model, the CEV model in its absolute diffusion form, the displaced diffusion model with a=.5 and a=1.5, the pure jump model, and the jump diffusion model are considered. Due to the reversal, none of the models is able to capture all the biases found. Conforming to the categorization table above, the compound option, absolute diffusion and a=1.5 displaced diffusion models perform well in the first period. Conversely, the a=.5 displaced diffusion and the pure jump model capture the reversed bias in the second period. The jump diffusion model performs poorly in both periods because it yields higher values for both in- and out-of-the-money options.[355]

Chapter 7.1. has already presented ample evidence on these switches in the striking price bias. This reversal is in fact the key to the assessment of any empirical evidence on model performance. Macbeth and Merville's (1980) work addressed above was conducted on the same 1976

---

[355] See Rubinstein (1985): op. cit., p. 478.

data that in an earlier test (Macbeth/Merville (1979), see Chapter 7.1.) revealed a consistent bias conforming to Rubinstein's first period. Therefore, their favorable result regarding the CEV model is no surprise. Recall that the year 1976 in fact coincides with part of Rubinstein's first period. The same is true for the data used in Beckers' (1980) test (above). His sample period ends in Sept. 1977, right before Rubinstein's reversal occurs.

Evidence on the reversal is corroborated in a study by Barone-Adesi (1986), who uses data for the entire year 1977 to study the performance of the compound option model. He does not find the compound option model to generally outperform the BS model. The reason is that he, too, finds the striking price bias in 1977 to reverse, although unlike Rubinstein, he cannot assign a particular date to the phenomenon.[356]

To date, empirical tests on the stochastic volatility model have not been performed. However, in light of the evidence presented above, the model would not automatically capture the bias reversal, either. It should be noted that both the displaced diffusion model and the stochastic volatility model can be specified as to capture

---

356 See Barone-Adesi, Giovanni: Maximum likelihood tests of option pricing models, in: Advances in Futures and Options Research, Volume 1 (1986), Part A, pp. 181-192, here p. 478.

either one of the biases. In Rubinstein's first period, the displaced diffusion model performs well with a>1, while the stochastic volatility model would require the specification of a negative correlation with the stock price. Conversely, the second period requires a<1 or positive correlation, respectively. However, the open question remains: what would signal the user of the model when to switch the specification, and to which level? So far, nobody has found an answer.[357]

The ability of the models to capture time to expiration biases has not been explicitly discussed in this chapter. Recall from Section 7.2. that empirical evidence finds biases pertaining to the time to expiration to be much more unclear than the striking price biases. Hence, it is no surprise that in Rubinstein's (1985a) test, no single model is able to capture all forms of maturity bias found during the sample period. In addition, the use of a model that corresponds to some time to expiration bias frequently worsens the performance regarding the prevailing striking price bias.[358]

---

[357] In theory, the displaced diffusion model could produce the reversal if the combination of risky assets, riskless assets, and the debt in the firm's capital structure is observed to change significantly. However, a sudden, substantial change in the debt level and asset composition is highly unlikely in the first place. In addition, it is very improbable to occur at the same time and in the same direction for the majority of the 30 stocks in Rubinstein's sample.

[358] See Rubinstein (1985): op. cit., p. 478.

8.5. Implications

The results on the performance of the models are disappointing. No single model can consistently outperform the BS model because the biases are unstable. In fact, all the painstaking theoretical work that resulted in the alternative models appears virtually in vain.

Given the complexity of the alternative models and the question of how to get the right values for their additional variables, the Black-Scholes model remains the prime candidate for use in practice. The only unequivocal improvement appears to be a dividend adjustment, either by using the pseudo-American formula or, slightly better but much more complex, the RGW model.

This result is not necessarily surprising. While the studies that consider the leverage effect (Schmalensee/Trippi (1978), Beckers (1980), Christie (1982)) confirm its existence, they also show that the leverage effect is insufficient to explain <u>all</u> changes in the volatility.[359] The leverage effect makes economical sense: the after-interest earnings pertaining to the stockholders fluctuate more widely the higher the

---

[359] See Schmalensee/Trippi (1978): op. cit., p. 141; Beckers (1980): op. cit., p. 665.; Christie (1982): op. cit., p. 428.

proportion of debt employed to finance the assets that generate those earnings. However, the strong tendency of ISD's to move together even after filtering out the leverage effect (see Section 8.1.) further supports the notion that a lot of other factors also have an impact. Could these marketwide influences, unrelated to the underlying stocks, sometimes dominate the leverage effect and hence cause the cross-over in the striking price bias?

The evidence on stock return distributions, too, (see Section 4.1.) shows that the prevalence of one particular bias should not be expected. Over longer periods of time, the distribution appears leptokurtic, i.e. both tails are fatter than in the normal distribution. Kon (1984) eliminates much of this behavior by dividing his 18-year sample into subperiods. He eventually concludes that the stock return distribution can best be explained by switches between a discrete number of normal distributions with different means and variances. Although Kon does not specifically address the following hypothesis, isn't it conceivable that these switches might result in the bias cross-overs?

Rubinstein (1985a) proposes that it might be promising to look for a correlation between the biases and some macroeconomic variables.[360] Kon suggests that changes in

---

[360] See Rubinstein (1985): op. cit., p. 479.

the variance may be due to changes in the stock's CAPM-beta with the market (firm-specific micro effects), as well as changes in the market's return variance as a whole (macro effects).[361]

Whatever the relationship may be, a composite option valuation model that identifies and incorporates it has yet to be developed.

[361]See Kon (1984): op. cit., p. 162.

9. WHERE DO WE GO FROM HERE?

The preceding chapters have presented ample evidence that option price deviations from BS don't give rise to abnormal return opportunities. Attempts to nonetheless improve the "fit" by developing more complex models that capture a specific bias have been shown to fail because of the bias reversals. Hence, the discussion has ultimately led us back full circle to where it started: the Black-Scholes model and its flaws. In the absence of better alternatives, how severe is the impact of transaction costs and all the other imperfections? Do they make the BS replication rationale so costly and risky that its applicability is questionable?

9.1. Transaction Cost Bounds Around Black-Scholes Values

Figlewski (1989) gives a rather pessimistic outlook on the explanatory power of the BS rationale. He examines the effect of various factors on the replicating strategy by simulating a lognormal price path for the underlying stock and calculating corresponding BS values. The lognormal simulation for the stock path rules out problems arising from deviations from Brownian motion. Equivalently, dividends, short sale restrictions, interest rate movements, and taxes are also left out.

The approach is to form hedge portfolios by buying (selling) the call and shorting (buying) the stock according to the hedge ratio Δ, which is calculated with the known volatility of .15 p.a. Subsequently, the excess hedge return (or cost) over and above the risk free rate of 5% p.a. is determined. Time to expiration is set at one month.

The impact of the remaining factors and imperfections that are examined is considerable:

* When hedging a correctly priced at-the-money call (i.e. the market price is assumed to equal the BS value), by rebalancing only once a day, the excess return is, as expected, zero. However, the discrete rebalancing results in a risky hedge with an annualized standard deviation of 6.52%, i.e. the hedge standard deviation is even higher than the risk free rate.
* If the hedger uses an incorrect volatility estimate, the Δ he computes is wrong, and hence the hedge return's standard deviation is even higher. In addition, he would of course risk to sell the call below its true value, thus locking in a loss.
* Indivisibilities significantly increase hedge risk as soon as the position size allows rebalancing only in

increments equivalent to one share or greater.[362]

* The required hedge investment (positive or negative) is very large, compared to the size of the profit opportunities that arise from mispricings. In an example, an at-the-money call with K=100 is mispriced by $.60 (which by the way corresponds to a considerable error in the volatility estimate: .10 instead of the true .15). To capture this mispricing of $.60, a hedge position worth more than $50 is required.[363]

* Implicit and explicit transaction costs (bid-ask spreads and fees) are path-dependent. The results show that rebalancing is required virtually every day, on average adding up to the equivalent of approximately five share transactions per hedge until expiration. A market maker who hedges the correctly-priced at-the-money call, initially worth about $2, would experience a considerable average $.27 loss when taking the author's estimate of transaction costs into account. Surprisingly, the hedge risk is hardly affected by the transaction costs. The average losses to a private investor, especially if he has to pay fixed minimum commissions, are far higher than the value of the option, thus making it futile to further

---

362 See Figlewski (1989): op. cit., pp. 1296-1298.

363 See ibid. p. 1295.

consider arbitrage opportunities such an investor faces.[364]

* Reducing costs by rebalancing less frequently does not yield significantly better results, either, because the incurred hedge risk rises.[365] The cost/risk results are in general shown to be somewhat better for rebalancing after a particular hedge ratio change compared to rebalancing after fixed intervals, but the differences are not overwhelming.[366]

* The hedging errors induce risk, and the transaction costs turn hedging of calls priced at BS value into losses. Covering them with a probability of 50% hence means that the trader will on average break even. The corresponding mispricing required to cover costs should hence be the minimum band around the option value within which no trader will take action. This band is considerable and is shown to widen the higher the profit probability is: above 50%, the standard deviation in the hedge return arising from the hedging error must be taken into account, thus widening the band. In the simulation, mispricings that allow a market maker to make a profit with a probability of 75% would have to be so large that

---

[364] See ibid. p. 1298.

[365] See ibid. pp. 1301-1302.

[366] Apart from the base case of daily rebalancing and the extreme case of no rebalancing at all, Figlewski examines rebalancing intervals of 2 and 5 days, as well as adjustments triggered by hedge ratio changes of .10 and .25.

they can even require violations of the call's lower bound $C \geq S-K$ (for underpricings)![367] The results are even more discouraging when options with longer maturities are considered.[368]

* An important observation is that the simulation bands are much wider than the bid-ask spreads actually quoted by options market makers on the CBOE. This indicates that market makers appear to be willing to buy and sell at prices within the bands. If hedging with the underlying stocks until expiration were the market makers' strategy in reality, buying or selling calls within the bands would result in considerable losses. The evidence hence implies that the standard BS replicating strategy <u>cannot be the main force</u> that drives option prices to where they are.[369]

The rather elaborate discussion of Figlewski's results serves to point out that it is justified to ask: Is the Black-Scholes model based on such an unrealistic strategy that its option values are virtually useless in practice?

Although not even considering many of the other factors

---

[367] Figlewski concedes that the impact of transaction costs is smaller in index options because they can be hedged with index futures, where transaction costs are about one tenth of those incurred for stocks. See p. 1308.

[368] See Figlewski (1989): op. cit., pp. 1303-1306.

[369] See ibid. p. 1307.

presented in this thesis, Figlewski does somewhat overstate the risk entailed in standard replication. As mentioned before, hedging errors for reasonable revision intervals are diversifiable. Hence, even for higher profit probabilities in the simulation, the band would remain at the 50% level, because the hedge risk could be ignored. However, this band is still very wide with daily rebalancing. For example, the at-the-money call in the simulation could be priced between $1.74 and $2.35 before giving rise to standard arbitrage opportunities.

Yet, hedging errors from less than daily rebalancing might still be diversifiable, resulting in less transaction costs and hence in a tighter range around the BS value. Also, (slightly) better results regarding costs versus hedge risk are shown to be obtainable when rebalancing only after a particular change in the hedge ratio. One should not forget, however, that the diversification requirement can conceivably only be met by a few active and well-capitalized market participants that constantly trade numerous positions.

Leland (1985) attacks discrete rebalancing and path dependent transaction costs by directly recognizing them in a modified hedging strategy. The BS model's volatility estimate is altered by incorporating a percentage round trip transaction cost rate and some discrete revision interval.[370] Despite the path-dependency of transaction costs, the resulting hedging errors including transaction costs are shown to be uncorrelated with stock price changes and therefore uncorrelated with the market.[371]

Leland's approach is appealing because it results in a direct analytical solution for symmetric upper and lower bounds around the theoretical Black-Scholes value. The bounds get wider when the transaction cost rate rises, or when the rebalancing interval gets shorter, or both. The widest bounds in dollar terms occur for at-the-money options because their hedge ratio is most sensitive to stock price changes, resulting in high stock turnover. In per cent of the option price, the bounds are widest for out-of-the-money options, because they are comparatively lower priced.[372]

Ultimately, the implication of both works above is the same: <u>transaction costs cause considerably wide bounds</u> around the theoretical option value within which the argument of arbitrage with a replicating portfolio is not applicable. This result is similar to the one already

---

[370] Discussed examples are .25%, 1%, 4% and 1 week, 4 weeks and 8 weeks, respectively.

[371] See Leland, Hayne E.: Option pricing and replication with transactions costs, in: JOF 40 (1985), pp. 1283-1301, here pp. 1289-1291.

[372] See ibid. pp. 1298-1300.

obtained earlier for the dominance bounds and arbitrage relationships.

Figure 9.a.: Transaction cost bounds around the BS values

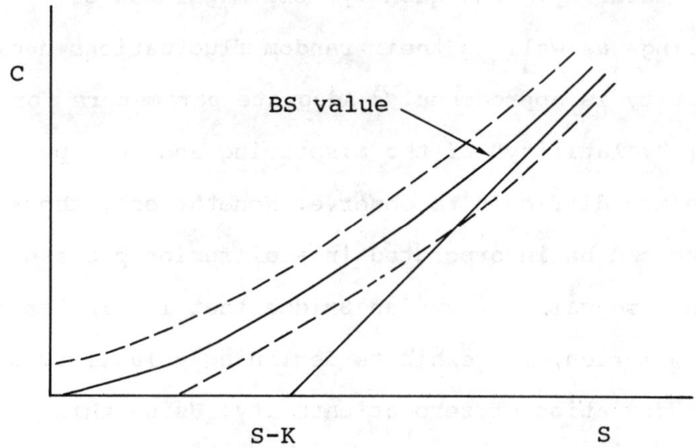

9.2. <u>Options Imbedded in an Arbitrage Portfolio</u>

A modified notion of arbitrage may alleviate the transaction cost effects. Mispricings in the market are not static. Positive and negative deviations from model values can fluctuate randomly until expiration, even switching sign. Hence, any arbitrageur who holds an arbitrage portfolio also holds an <u>early closeout option</u> imbedded in it. If the mispricing changes in the opposite direction, the trader can unwind the hedge early, realizing a higher arbitrage profit in a shorter period of time than when holding the hedge until option maturity.

The value of the early closeout option can be determined by considering that the mispricing has to be zero at maturity. Consequently, the magnitude of mispricings as well as their random fluctuations decline as maturity is approached.[373] Adequate parameters for the initial "volatility" of the mispricing and the speed of decline are difficult to observe. Nonetheless, these features can be incorporated in a diffusion process, for example a so-called Brownian Bridge that is similar to Brownian motion, but exhibits declining volatility and a certain deviation of zero at maturity. Using this rationale makes it possible to derive a value for the early closeout option.[374]

Considering the value of this imbedded option, an arbitrage trade may well be attractive even if the mispricing lies within the transaction cost bounds described above. One must point out that such a strategy is not riskless because the mispricing may eventually behave in a way that the hedge must be held until expiration, resulting in an after transaction cost

---

[373] See Mello, Antonio S.: Stock index arbitrage with early unwinding opportunities, working paper, Dec. 1988., pp. 6-7;
Duffie, Darrell: The risk neutral value of the early arbitrage option, Stanford University working paper, June 1987, p.2.

[374] See Mello (1988): op. cit., p. 14; Duffie (1987): op. cit., p. 3.

loss.[375]

If the random fluctuation in the mispricing is uncorrelated with the stock and hence the market, this risk should again be diversifiable in a portfolio context. However, the existence of the systematic pricing biases indicates that this is probably not the case. For example, in a period where the BS model on average underprices out-of-the-money calls and overprices in-the-money calls, a positive market price deviation on an out-of-the-money call is obviously more likely to disappear when it moves into the money, i.e. when the stock price rises.

Coupled with the early closeout option is the <u>option to reestablish</u>. If the mispricing switches sign, it is possible to establish a reversed hedge position. If the mispricing reappears with the same sign shortly after early closeout, the original hedge can be reestablished.

The early closeout option and the reestablish option in effect raise the return achievable on a particular hedge investment over a particular time. While approaches for their theoretical valuation are still in an early stage, they appear to be the major factor that can imply a significant compression of the transaction cost bounds.

Recall from Chapter 7 that a number of trading strategies testing the profitability of mispricing

---

[375] See Mello (1988): op. cit, p. 18.

arbitrage included early closeouts and position reestablishing. Yet, none of them yielded abnormal returns. This indicates that the effective mispricings found in the markets conform to bounds that are tighter than those implied by Leland's (1985) and especially Figlewski's (1989) work. Figlewski's observation that his simulated bounds are far wider than the bid-ask spread quoted by option market makers hints in the same direction.

9.3. Quasi Arbitrage

A final consideration is the possibility of quasi arbitrage. It denotes activities of investors who actually seek net positions in a security, but synthesize it if mispricings make a replicating portfolio cheaper than the direct position.[376]

Holding calls and lending replicates a position in stocks. Holding calls and shorting stocks is equivalent to borrowing, and so on. Investors who desire a particular position in stocks or bonds can synthesize it by using an option and one of the other two securities. If the option is mispriced by the market, this can cost less than establishing the direct position.

---

[376] See Siegel, Daniel R. / Siegel, Diane F.: Futures Markets, Orlando, Fl. 1990, p. 72.

Quasi arbitrageurs hence save the transaction costs on the initial offsetting position in the third security that pure arbitrageurs establish in order to make profits on zero net investment. Unfortunately, the rebalancing requirement for the BS replicating portfolio will render these initial savings relatively negligible. Quasi arbitrage hence won't significantly compress the transaction cost bounds around option values. However, it is conceivable that bounds around the put-call parity can be reduced because it does not entail rebalancing, thus making cost savings in one of the four participating securities a significant factor.

One has to keep in mind that quasi arbitrageurs, unlike pure arbitrageurs, will not engage in their activities to an unlimited extent. They will stop when they have reached their desired net position. Hence, the force of quasi arbitrage compared to pure arbitrage should be much weaker.[377]

---

[377] See ibid. p. 77.

10. CONCLUSION

This thesis has presented ample evidence that the costly and risky trading environment in real markets substantially weakens the arbitrage arguments that are the basis for all preference-free option valuation theories.

Market imperfections and nonaccordance with assumptions cause considerable bounds around dominance conditions, arbitrage relationships, and model values. While these very bounds make it impossible to reject the validity of the Black-Scholes (or any other) option valuation model, they also significantly reduce its usefulness for day to day trading.

The key to this dilemma is the difference between value and price. Although the Black-Scholes model may well be a good approach to determine the fair value of an option, its actual market price can fluctuate anywhere within the bounds. Within these bounds, anything can drive the option price, but **not** standard arbitrage with the replicating portfolio.

Traders consciously take risks when dealing inside the bounds, often hedging with other options (whose price can again deviate), or taking short-term net positions in the hope that they can be sold with a profit.[378] It can be perfectly appropriate for a trader to buy an overpriced option within the bounds if he believes that it will stay overpriced for a while. Expectations and risk aversion (e.g. CPRA) can play a substantial role inside the bounds, where the elegant arbitrage arguments that allow risk neutral valuation and independence from the stock's expected return cannot be applied.

The systematic behavior of deviations from Black-Scholes values has prompted extensive research to develop amendments to the Black-Scholes framework. Yet, the resulting models are shown to perform inadequately when the biases reverse.

The complexity of the market environment will further challenge academia, but in the absence of proven superior alternatives, the Black-Scholes model so far remains the benchmark approach for the option valuation problem. However, its capability to accurately determine market prices and to explain how they got to where they are is limited.

Finally, the evidence presented here underscores the economic usefulness of traded options. For one, they are a means of information conveyance that reduces stock

---

[378] See Figlewski (1989): op. cit., p. 1307.

volatility. More importantly, they enable any investor to acquire their payoff pattern at a price whose deviations from some fair value are confined to the costs and risks borne by the most advantageously placed trader. Many market participants would be deprived of this investment opportunity if traded options didn't exist: their replication would be too risky and costly for most of them.

GLOSSARY

a) List of Variables

This alphabetical list of variables encompasses all variables that are frequently used throughout the thesis. It does not contain the variables that are specifically defined for only one particular concept or option valuation model. These specific variables are defined in the specific context and can also be found in appendix 3, which summarizes the alternatives to the Black-Scholes model that are discussed in this thesis.

c = value of a European call option

C = value of an American call option

CCRR= continuously compounded rate of return

d = downward stock return over a period of arbitrary length

D = cash dividend

dt = infinitessimally small time increment

dz = Wiener process

e_j = price of a state-contingent claim

F = face value of debt

K = striking price

N(d)= probability that a standardized normally distributed random variable will be less than or equal to d (cumulative normal density function)

p = value of a European put option, except when denoting pseudo-probabilities in the binomial model

P = value of an American put option

r = annualized continuously compounded risk-free interest rate

R = risk-free return over a period of arbitrary length

S = current stock price

S^* = stock price at option maturity

t = time to option maturity, computed from now

t_i = time to a specific date (e.g. dividend payment) before maturity, computed from now

T = some time period different from t; starting now

u = upward stock return over a period of arbitrary length

V = current value of the firm

V_j = future stock price in state j

x = personal income tax rate

δ = continuously compounded fixed dividend yield

Δ = hedge ratio, except when used to denote a change in the value of variables over a time increment

λ = proportion of a particular option in a portfolio of options; $0 \leq \lambda \leq 1$

Λ = sensitivity of an option to volatility changes

μ = certain drift in Brownian motion

ρ = correlation coefficient

σ = standard deviation (volatility) of the continuously compounded rate of return (CCRR) of the stock

σ_V = volatility of the firm value

τ = some time interval of specific length; does not necessarily start now

b) <u>List of Abbreviations for Academic Journals</u>

FAJ = Financial Analysts Journal

FM = Financial Management

JOB = Journal of Business

JOF = Journal of Finance

JFQA= Journal of Financial and Quantitative Analysis

JFEC= Journal of Financial Economics

c) <u>Other Abbreviations</u>

BS = Black-Scholes

CBOE= Chicago Board Options Exchange

CEV = constant elasticity of variance (option valuation model)

ISD = implied σ when equating market prices with Black-Scholes model values

NYSE= New York Stock Exchange

OCC = Option Clearing Corporation

OTC = over-the-counter (option market)

RGW = Roll-Geske-Whaley (option valuation model)

APPENDIX 1: Summary of Bounds on Option Values

Where applicable in the relationships below, $K_1<K_2$ and $t_1<t_2$. The bracket (...) denotes variables of which the option value is a function.

Bounds on Call Values:

* $S \geq C \geq c \geq 0$
* $c \geq \max[0, S-Ke^{-rt}-PV(D)]$ (can be $\gtrless$ S-K)
* $C \geq \max[0, S-Ke^{-rt}-PV(D), S-K]$
* $c(K_1) \geq c(K_2)$
* $C(K_1) \geq C(K_2)$
* $c(K_1)-c(K_2) \leq (K_2-K_1)e^{-rt}$
* $C(K_1)-C(K_2) \leq (K_2-K_1)$
* $c(t_2) \geq c(t_1)$ if no dividend paid between t_1 and t_2.
* $C(t_2) \geq C(t_1)$

Bounds on Put Values

* $K \geq P \geq p \geq 0$, $p \leq Ke^{-rt}$
* $p \geq \max[0, Ke^{-rt}-S+PV(D)]$ (can be $\gtrless$ K-S)
* $P \geq \max[0, Ke^{-rt}-S+PV(D), K-S]$
* $p(K_2) \geq p(K_1)$
* $P(K_2) \geq P(K_1)$
* $p(K_2)-p(K_1) \leq (K_2-K_1)e^{-rt}$
* $P(K_2)-P(K_1) \leq (K_2-K_1)$
* $p(t_2) \geq p(t_1)$ but only if having more time to get into the money is worth more than the loss of interest on K caused by longer maturity; usually, the stock volatility is high enough to create sufficient value for having more time to get into the money.
* $P(t_2) \geq P(t_1)$ which always holds: the problem above for European puts arises at the critical stock price below which early exercise is optimal; thus, early exercise prevents longer maturity American puts from being worth less than with shorter maturity.

APPENDIX 2: The Roll-Geske-Whaley (RGW) Formula

For the value of an American call on a stock with a single known dividend paid before option maturity, the formula is:

$$C = S[N_1(b_1) + N_2(a_1, -b_1; -\sqrt{\frac{t_D}{t}})] - Ke^{-rt}[N_1(b_2)e^{r(t-t_D)} + N_2(a_2, -b_2; -\sqrt{\frac{t_D}{t}})]$$
$$+ \alpha De^{-rt_D}N_1(b_2)$$

where

$$a_1 = \frac{\ln(\frac{S}{K}) + (r+\frac{1}{2}\sigma^2)t}{\sigma\sqrt{t}}, \qquad a_2 = a_1 - \sigma\sqrt{t},$$

$$b_1 = \frac{\ln(\frac{S}{S_D}) + (r+\frac{1}{2}\sigma^2)t_D}{\sigma\sqrt{t_D}}, \qquad b_2 = b_1 - \sigma\sqrt{t_D}$$

Notation not previously specified:

t_D = time until the ex-dividend date
t = time to maturity of the American call
S = the current stock price, <u>net</u> of escrowed dividend
S_D = the solution to $C(S_D, t-t_D, K) = S_D + \alpha D - K$, where $C(.)$ is the original BS value
σ = volatility of the annualized CCRR on S
D = the cash dividend
α = the known decline in the stock price at the ex-dividend date as a proportion of the dividend
$N_1(.)$ = univariate cumulative normal distribution function
$N_2(a,b;\rho)$ = bivariate cumulative normal distribution function with upper integral limits a and b and correlation coefficient ρ, i.e. the cumulative probability that the first variable is less than a and the second variable is less than b when the correlation coefficient between the variables is ρ

APPENDIX 3: Option Valuation Formulas for Changing Stock Volatilities and for Jump Processes

1. The Compound Option Formula

For the value of a European call on a non-dividend-paying stock, the formula is:

$$c = VN_2(h+\sigma_V\sqrt{t}, k+\sigma_V\sqrt{T}; \sqrt{\frac{T}{t}}) - Fe^{-rT}N_2(h,k;\sqrt{\frac{T}{t}}) - Ke^{-rt}N_1(h)$$

where

$$h = \frac{\ln(\frac{V}{\bar{V}}) + (r-\frac{1}{2}\sigma_V^2)t}{\sigma_V\sqrt{t}},$$

$$k = \frac{\ln(\frac{V}{F}) + (r-\frac{1}{2}\sigma_V^2)T}{\sigma_V\sqrt{T}}, \qquad \text{and}$$

$\bar{V}$ = that value of V such that

$S_t - K = Vn_1(k+\sigma_V\sqrt{(T-t)}) - Fe^{-rt}N_1(k) - K = 0$

Notation not previously specified:

- t = time to maturity of the call
- T = time to maturity of the debt, $T>t$
- F = face value of the debt
- V = value of the firm
- σ_V = volatility of the firm
- $N_1(.)$ = univariate cumulative normal distribution function
- $N_2(.)$ = bivariate cumulative normal distribution function with h and k as upper integral limits and $\sqrt{t/T}$ as the correlation coefficient

2. The CEV-Absolute Diffusion Formula

For the value of a European call on a non-dividend-paying stock, the formula is:

$$c = (S-Ke^{-rt})N(y_1) + (S-Ke^{-rt})N(y_2) + v[n(y_1)-n(y_2)]$$

where

$$v = \sigma\sqrt{\frac{1-e^{-2rt}}{2r}},$$

$$y_1 = \frac{S-Ke^{-rt}}{v},$$

$$y_2 = \frac{-S-Ke^{-rt}}{v}, \quad \text{and}$$

$$n(y) = \frac{1}{\sqrt{2\pi}}e^{-\frac{y^2}{2}}$$

3. The Displaced Diffusion Formula

For the value of a European call on a non-dividend-paying stock, the formula is:

$$c = aSN(d_1) - (K-bS)e^{-rt}N(d_2)$$

where

$$d_1 = \frac{\ln(\frac{aS}{K-bS})+(r-\frac{\sigma_{risk}^2}{2})t}{\sigma_{risk}\sqrt{t}},$$

$$d_2 = d_1-\sigma_{risk}\sqrt{t}, \quad \text{and}$$

$$a = \alpha(1+\beta)$$
$$b = (1-a)e^{rt}$$

Notation not previously specified:

α = initial risky proportion of total assets
β = initial debt-to-equity ratio
σ_{risk} = volatility of the risky assets
If there are known dividends, their value, compounded to maturity at the risk-free rate, is subtracted from b.

4. The Pure Jump Formula

For the value of a European call on a non-dividend-paying stock, the formula is:

$$c = S\Psi(x;y) - Ke^{-rt}\Psi(x,\frac{y}{u})$$

where

$$\Psi(\alpha;\beta) = \sum_{i=\alpha}^{\infty} \frac{e^{-\beta}\beta^{i}}{i!},$$

$$y = \frac{(r+w)tu}{u-1}, \quad \text{and}$$

x is the smallest nonnegative integer greater than

$$\frac{\ln(\frac{K}{S})+wt}{\ln(u)}$$

Notation not previously specified:

u = discrete jump return of the stock; u>1
w = continuously compounded decline rate of the stock

5. The Jump Diffusion Formula

In the simplest form of the jump diffusion model, the logarithm of the size of the proportional jump has a normal distribution. Assuming the standard deviation of that normal distribution is ς, the formula for a European call on a non-dividend-paying stock is:

$$c = \sum_{n=0}^{\infty} \frac{e^{-\gamma' t}(\gamma' t)^n}{n!} f_n$$

where

γ' = $\gamma(1+k)$, and

f_n = the Black-Scholes option price where the instantaneous variance rate is

$$\sigma^2 + \frac{n\varsigma^2}{t}$$

and the risk-free rate is

$$r - \gamma k + \frac{n[\ln(1+k)]}{t}$$

Notation not previously specified:

γ = jump occurrence rate
k = average jump size as a proportional increase in the stock price

REFERENCES

1. Barone-Adesi, Giovanni (1986): Maximum likelihood tests of option pricing models, in: Advances in Futures and Options Research, volume 1, part A, pages 181-192.

2. Beaver, William (1968): The information content of annual earnings announcements, in: Empirical research in accounting, supplement to the Journal of Accounting Research 6, pages 67-92.

3. Beckers, Stan (1980): The constant elasticity of variance model and its implications for option pricing, in: Journal of Finance 35, pages 661-673.

4. Beckers, Stan (1981): Standard deviations implied in option prices as predictors of future stock price variability, in: Journal of Banking and Finance 5, pages 161-185.

5. Bhattacharya, Mihir (1983): Transactions data tests of efficiency of the Chicago Board Options Exchange, in: Journal of Financial Economics 12, pages 161-185.

6. Black, Fischer (1975): Fact and fantasy in the use of options, in: Financial Analysts Journal (July-August), pages 36-72.

7. Black, Fischer / Scholes, Myron (1972): The valuation of option contracts and a test of market efficiency, papers and proceedings of the thirtieth annual meeting of the American Finance Association, 17-29 Dec. 1971, in: Journal of Finance 27, pages 399-417.

8. Black, Fischer / Scholes, Myron (1973): The pricing of options and corporate liabilities, in: Journal of Political Economy 81, pages 637-654.

9. Blattberg, Robert / Gonedes, Nicholas (1974): A comparison of the stable and student distributions as statistical models for stock prices, in: Journal of Business 47, pages 244-280.

10. Bodie,Zvi / Kane, Alex / Marcus, Alan J.: Investments, Boston 1989.

11. Boyle, Phelim P. / Emanuel, David (1980): Discretely adjusted option hedges, in: Journal of Financial Economics 8, pages 259-282.

12. Chance, Don M. (1986): Empirical tests of the pricing of index call options, in: Advances in Futures and Options Research, volume 1, part A, pages 141-166.

13. Chance, Don M.: An Introduction to Options and Futures, Chicago 1989.

14. Chicago Board Options Exchange: Fundamental Facts about the World's Largest Options Marketplace (current booklet).

15. Chicago Board Options Exchange: S+P 100 Index Options: The Index Edge, Chicago 1988.

16. Chicago Board Options Exchange: Fee Schedule as of July 1, 1989.

17. Chiras, Donald P. / Manaster, Steven (1978): The information content of option prices and a test of market efficiency, in: Journal of Financial Economics 6, pages 213-234.

18. Christie, Andrew A. (1982): The stochastic behavior of common stock variances, in: Journal of Financial Economics 10, pages 145-166.

19. Cox, John C. / Ross, Stephen A. (1976): The valuation of options for alternative stochastic processes, in: Journal of Financial Economics 3, pages 145-166.

20. Cox, John C. / Ross, Stephen A. / Rubinstein, Mark (1979): Option pricing: a simplified approach, in: Journal of Financial Economics 7, pages 229-263.

21. Cox, John C. / Rubinstein, Mark: Options Markets, Englewood Cliffs 1985.

22. Duffie, Darrell (1987): The risk neutral value of the early arbitrage option, Stanford University Working Paper, June 1987.

23. Duffie, Darrell: Futures Markets, Englewood Cliffs 1989.

24. Fidelity Investments: Commission Schedule 1989.

25. Figlewski, Stephen (1989a): Options arbitrage in imperfect markets, in: Journal of Finance 44, pages 1289-1311.

26. Figlewski, Stephen (1989b): What does an option pricing model tell us about option prices?, in: Financial Analysts Journal (September-October), pages 12-15.

27. Galai, Dan (1977): Tests of market efficiency of the Chicago Board Options Exchange, in: Journal of Business 50, pages 167-197.

28. Galai, Dan (1978): Empirical tests of boundary conditions for CBOE options, in: Journal of Financial Economics 6, pages 187-211.

29. Galai, Dan (1979): A convexity test for traded options, in: Quarterly Review of Economics and Business 19, pages 83-90.

30. Galai, Dan (1983): A survey of empirical tests of option pricing models, in: Option Pricing: Theory and Applications, edited by Menachem Brenner, Heath 1983, pages 45-80.

31. Gastineau, Gary L. (1988): The time has come to eliminate option position limits, in: Financial Analysts Journal (July-August), pages 7-8.

32. Geske, Robert (1978): The pricing of options with stochastic dividend yield, in Journal of Finance 33, pages 617-625.

33. Geske, Robert (1979a): The valuation of compound options, in: Journal of Financial Economics 7, pages 63-81.

34. Geske, Robert (1979b): A note on an analytical valuation formula for unprotected American call options on stocks with known dividends, in: Journal of Financial Economics 7, pages 375-380.

35. Geske, Robert / Roll, Richard (1984): On valuing American call options with the Black-Scholes European formula, in: Journal of Finance 39, pages 443-455.

36. Gilster, John E. / Lee, William (1984): The effects of transaction costs and different borrowing and lending rates on the option pricing model: a note, in: Journal of Finance 39, pages 1215-1221.

37. Gladstein, Mathew L. / Merton, Robert C. / Scholes, Myron (1982): The returns and risks of alternative put-option investment strategies, in: Journal of Business 55, pages 1-55.

38. Gould, J.P. / Galai, Dan (1974): Transaction costs and the relationship between put and call prices, in: Journal of Financial Economics 1, pages 105-129.

39. Grossman, Sanford J. (1988): An analysis of the implications for stock and futures price volatility of program trading and dynamic hedging strategies, in: Journal of Business 61, pages 275-298.

40. Hayes, Samuel L. / Tennenbaum, Michael E. (1979): The impact of listed options on the underlying shares, in: Financial Management 8, pages 72-77.

41. Heaton, Hal (1986): Options and tax clienteles, in: Advances in Futures and Options Research, volume 1, part A, pages 167-179.

42. Ho, Thomas S. / Macris, Richard G. (1984): Dealer bid-ask quotes and transaction prices: an empirical study of some AMEX options, in: Journal of Finance 39, pages 23-45.

43. Hull, John: Options, Futures and other Derivative Securities, Englewood Cliffs 1989.

44. Hull, John / White, Alan (1988): An analysis of the bias in option pricing caused by a stochastic volatility, in: Advances in Futures and Options Research, volume 3, pages 29-61.

45. Klemkosky, Robert C. / Resnik, Bruce G. (1980): An ex ante analysis of put-call parity, in: Journal of Financial Economics 8, pages 363-378.

46. Kon, Stanley J. (1984): Models of stock returns-a comparison, in: Journal of Finance 39, pages 147-165.

47. Latané, Henry A. / Rendleman, Richard J. (1976): Standard deviations of stock price ratios implied in option premia, in: Journal of Finance 31, pages 369-381.

48. Leland, Hayne E. (1985): Option pricing and replication with transactions costs, in: Journal of Finance 40, pages 1283-1301.

49. Macbeth, James D. / Merville, Larry J. (1979): An empirical examination of the Black-Scholes call option pricing model, in: Journal of Finance 34, pages 1173-1186.

50. Macbeth, James D. / Merville, Larry J. (1980): Tests of the Black-Scholes and Cox call option valuation models, in: Journal of Finance 35, pages 285-301.

51. Marshall, John F.: Futures and Option Contracting, Cincinnati 1989.

52. Mello, Antonio S. (1988): Stock index arbitrage with early unwinding opportunities, Working Paper Dec. 1988.

53. Merton, Robert C. (1973): Theory of rational option pricing, in: Bell Journal of Economics and Management Science 4, pages 141-183.

54. Merton, Robert C. (1976): Option pricing when underlying stock returns are discontinuous, in: Journal of Financial Economics 3, pages 125-144.

55. Merton, Robert C. (1977): On the pricing of contingent claims and the Modigliani-Miller theorem, in: Journal of Financial Economics 5, pages 241-249.

56. Patell, James / Wolfson, Mark (1981): The ex ante and ex post price effects of quarterly earnings announcemants reflected in option and stock prices, in: Journal of Accounting Research 19, pages 434-458.

57. Phillips, Susan M. / Smith, Clifford W. (1980): Trading costs for listed options, in: Journal of Financial Economics 8, pages 179-201.

58. Pratt, John W. (1964): Risk aversion in the small and in the large, in: Econometrica 32, pages 122-136.

59. Roll, Richard (1977): An analytic valuation formula for unprotected American call options on stocks with known dividends, in: Journal of Financial Economics 5, pages 251-258.

60. Ronn Aimee G. / Ronn, Ehud I. (1989): The box spread arbitrage condition: Theory, tests and investment strategies, in: Review of Financial Studies 2, pages 91-108.

61. Ross, Stephen A. (1976): Options and efficiency, in: Quarterly Journal of Economics 90, pages 75-89.

62. Ross, Stephen A. / Westerfield, Randolph W.: Corporate Finance, St. Louis 1988.

63. Ritchken, Peter H.: Options: Theory, Strategy and Applications, Glenview, Ill. 1987.

64. Ritchken, Peter H. (1985): On option pricing bounds, in: Journal of Finance 40, pages 1219-1233.

65. Rubinstein, Mark (1976): The valuation of uncertain income streams and the pricing of options, in: Bell Journal of Economics 7, pages 407-425.

66. Rubinstein, Mark (1983): Displaced diffusion option pricing, in: Journal of Finance 38, pages 213-217.

67. Rubinstein, Mark (1985a): Nonparametric tests of alternative option pricing models using all reported trades and quotes on the 30 most active CBOE option classes from August 23, 1976 through August 31, 1978, in: Journal of Finance 40, pages 455-480.

68. Rubinstein, Mark (1985b): Alternative paths to portfolio insurance, in: Financial Analysts Journal (July-August), pages 42-52.

69. Rubinstein, Mark (1988): Portfolio insurance and the market crash, in: Financial Analysts Journal (January-February), pages 38-47.

70. Siegel, Daniel R. / Siegel, Diane F.: Futures Markets, Orlando 1990.

71. Schmalensee, Richard / Trippi, Robert R. (1978): Common stock volatility expectations implied by option premia, in: Journal of Finance 33, pages 129-147.

72. Scholes, Myron (1976): Taxes and the pricing of options, in: Journal of Finance 31, pages 319-332.

73. Schmidt, Rainer H.: Grundzüge der Investitions- und Finanzierungstheorie, Wiesbaden, FRG, 1983.

74. Smidt, Seymour (1968): A new look at the random walk hypothesis, in: Journal of Financial and Quantitative Analysis, pages 235-261.

75. Smith, Clifford W. (1976): Option pricing, in: Journal of Financial Economics 3, pages 3-51.

76. Sterk, William E. (1983a): Comparative performance of the Black-Scholes and Roll-Geske-Whaley option pricing models, in: Journal of Financial and Quantitative Analysis 18, pages 345-354.

77. Sterk, William E. (1983b): Option pricing: dividends and the in- and out-of-the-money bias, in: Financial Management (Winter), pages 47-53.

78. Thorp, Edward (1973): Extensions of the Black-Scholes option model, in: Proceedings of the 39th session of the International Statistical Institute, Vienna, Austria, August 1973.

79. Trippi, Robert R. (1977): A test of option market efficiency using a random walk valuation model, in: Journal of Economics and Business 29, pages 93-98.

80. Westerfield, Randolph W. (1977): The distribution of common stock price changes: an application of transactions time and subordinated stochastic models, in: Journal of Financial and Quantitative Analysis 12, pages 743-765.

81. Whaley, Robert E. (1981): On the valuation of American call options on stocks with known dividends, in: Journal of Financial Economics 9, pages 207-211.